"Lawrence's Book, CREAM RISE~~~~~~~~~~~~~~~~~~~~~~~~~~~~ analysis of what it takes to rise to the top in the fitness industry. With vision and passion, Lawrence shares his deep understanding of health, wellness and career choices."
--*Sara Kooperman, JD, CEO, SCW Fitness Education, CEO, Les Mills Midwest*

"...a bright young youth who is a true guru in fitness"
--*Regis Philbin, host, "LIVE! with Regis and Kelly"*

"Lawrence continuously strives to empower others to express their untapped true inner potential. How fitting Lawrence has written a book about communicating because he truly is an outstanding communicator."
--*Constance Towers, castmember, ABC TV's General Hospital*

"Lawrence takes complex information and makes it simple, clear, and easy to understand. This is his brilliance as an instructor and educator and a true gift he so generously shares from those lucky enough stand in his glow."
--*Keli Roberts, Owner, Keli's Real Fitness, INC., and Gatorade Fit Series Spokesperson*

" Lawrence's insights and advice give anyone the tools they need to succeed and the wisdom to further their life. When I choose programs that help teachers learn how to teach, I always choose Lawrence among my faculty for this purpose. He has a gift."
--*Carol Scott, Owner, East Coast Alliance and IDEA Award Recipient*

"No one inspires me more than this author, Lawrence Biscontini. There's a true sense of genuine qualities and insight that motivates me to always seek ways to be the very best. I have all of my instructors read this book once when they start working for me"
--*Deborah Puskarich, Group Fitness Manager for Cooper Craig Ranch in Texas*

A true leader and teacher affects eternity; he can never tell where his influence stops. Lawrence is a such a leader and teacher... His influence continues to be global. His vision and passion have a profound influence on me as an international fitness & dance professional... He continues to share his elite wealth of knowledge here with his book; *Cream Rises* is a must read."
--*Calvin Wiley, Global Director & Founder of LEAD® & CALVINOGRAPHY®*

CREAM RISES: EXCELLENCE IN EDUCATION

3

findLawrence.com

Cream Rises: Excellence in Education
© 2011 by Lawrence Biscontini, MA
Version 10

Printed in the United States of America

Library of Congress Catalog Card Number:
ISBN: 978-0-578-03119-4

Published by: FG2000 and Lulu.com

All rights reserved. The author freely grants permission to
cite from this work for critical study, review, and dialogue.

4

DEDICATION

I dedicate this book to all of the talent that fills these pages, on the stages of my co-presenters joy or in the hearts of any convention delegate attending any of my sessions. My role here simply has been that of a sponge, soaking in all of the expertise of all of you and amalgamating those lessons into my own style. I hope to think I serve as but a mirror, reflecting the lessons of education and entertainment I have gathered since starting in 1983.

GRATITUDE:

I humbly thank God for infinite blessings, inspiration, and energy, and Constance Mary Towers, the apotheosis of impromptu grace and elocution (for her unending understanding, eloquence, and positivism). I also thank: Alana (for the "support and Scrabbles"); Maria Gavin; Sara Kooperman (for the Mania madness & opportunities); Petra Kolber (for the professional advice); C Mark Rees (for FG2000), the entire Golden Door Puerto Rico team; Stephanie Montgomery and Lisa Wheeler; AFAA (especially Laurie and Lisa), ACE; AEA (especially Julie and Angie); the AFPP (especially Tina Juan, Shirley, Earl, and Bam!); Mike and Stephanie Morris (for the teamwork on the BALL); Len Kravitz (for the mentoring and research); the gals at John and Ankie's Bodywork Gym in Mykonos, who had more of an open mind to everything than I ever thought possible; Diane Berson and J Sklar (for the details); Susan L. Fischer (for transcendence in education); Tom Snow (for the original "Yo-Chi" music for those early mind-body walks), Robert Milazzo (for the photos); the Xerox Queen herself, Maria Kalofolia (for the truest friendship); Ankie and John (for the Bodywork Gym hours); Kathie and Peter Davis for IDEA; Maureen Hagan for the Canadian fun at CanFitPro; Carol for ECA; Bernard Hasse (for the Hasenhau); Irene "Cathy" Narvaez (for the hundreds of e-mails as a premium personal assistant); Liz Kalmanowicz (for keeping the money flowing); Kathy Shelton (my first friend) for the first inspiration of excitement in my life and partner in 'crime' in documenting excellence in service; Deborah (in the expo), Lyndsay Murray-Kashoid for the great editing assistance; Yury Rockit Miankovich for lessons learned, Joseph, Dioni, and Ivy for accepting me so fully into the Salachas family in Halara, all of the colleagues who have come to any fitness session of mine at any convention anywhere; and Barbara.

TABLE OF CONTENTS

Welcome to the little Cream Rises: Excellence in Education book.

This book comes from two main sources. First, when I teach workshops and give lectures, I find that I oftentimes tell the same stories regardless of the actual topics at hand. It would seem that my story, as it were, is larger than any one topic that I'm presenting at any one time. I repeatedly notice that participants oftentimes take notes from these stories in addition to taking notes on the actual topics themselves. They write down *what* I have to say: these little stories that help illustrate my points in fitness.

Second, perhaps because I have a degree in education, perhaps because people flatter me when they compliment *how* I teach, I have decided to compile here my inspirations, resources, background thought processes, and my actual techniques illustrating *how* I teach.

This book puts together, then, both "WHAT" I teach, and, even more importantly, "HOW" I teach it. Since all educational processes can be summarized into these two categories, these will be the sections of this book. If you are a personal trainer or group fitness instructor, you will agree that nobody really ever creates a new movement. The "*what*," as it were, is already defined. What separates mediocrity from excellence, then, is really the "*how*." Approach is everything.

In our jobs, we learn on the spot each day what the "demons" and "controls" are.

9

By "demons" I mean the issues over which we have no control, like the expectations of people, the number of individuals who choose to come to class, the logistics, materials, and architecture of a specific room, the layout of the facility, and the general equipment available. By "controls" I mean everything else. This book really comes about as a dedication to the wide variety of aspects of each class that we can, in fact, manage. Putting careful study into as many *controllable* aspects of a class as possible helps the cream rise in creating excellence in education.

WHAT DOES 'TEACHING' REALLY MEAN?

Before detailing these two categories of "what" and "how," however, we should all begin with the same framework. To understand "excellence in education," we have first to understand a few terms. The word "education" actually comes from "teaching," which means "to bring about an independent change in behavior." Truly, if we are able to affect someone's behavior so much that, when we are no longer around, that person continues to produce a new action, thought, or behavior, we have *taught* something. If participants look great in a room as long as we are also demonstrating movement along with them, for example, and cannot reproduce such movement without us, theirs may be more like the role of the monkey or parrot in the circus. Our definition of teaching means that we can get most participants to be able to reproduce most movement without us.

Education refers to getting others to change something—and repeat it independently—that would not have occurred without intervention. We educate via communication, which I like to define as the "response you get regardless of your intention." Truly, many times we have preconceived in our head what we want to hear or see, but what we get is slightly or largely different. Imagine two individuals who don't speak each other's language deciding what to eat in a restaurant whose menu neither is able to read. Whatever they end up eating is a result of their ability to communicate to others what they would like to ingest.

The science of neurolinguistic programming (neurolinguisticprogramming.com) tells us that communication is only 7% words, 38% tone, and rest body language. Try to remember that when we go through dozens of practical examples in this book to realize the importance of what we DO over what we actually SAY, we aim at education. You probably have heard it said that "actions speak louder than words," and that "more important than what you say is what you do," but now there is a science dedicated to proving the adequacy of these two ancient adages.

The title came to me years ago when I was privileged enough to be watching Mindy

Mylrea teach as a guest instructor for me at the Golden Door Spa in Puerto Rico. I realized that she was truly a world great in terms of education and managing any type of group. I told her that she was the cream of cream of motivational group leaders. And it dawned on me that one of the most important differences between being good and being great is like milk or soy milk. They do a body good. A good instructor is effective, safe, and a good leader. Like milk, he or she does a body good. But cream, however, rises to the top and is exclusive, rich, expensive, tasty, selective, more rare, and smooth. Likewise, these adjectives describe a truly great leader. By definition and formula, cream rises to the top.

I invite you to imagine for a moment a world-class facility with eye-scanners for entrance cards, mood-lit movement studios with controllable aromatherapy and lighting at the touch of a button, heated pools with underwater multi-colored lights and speakers, a world-class spa, the best of all fitness equipment for all types of movement classes, outdoor organic trees that grow fruit picked individually for each juice bar smoothie, complimentary massage chairs for all members on a daily basis in a dark relaxation room, oversized plush white towels and robes in all lockers, daily laundry service and grocery shopping done for you while you attend classes, and $5 dollars direct deposited to your bank for every movement class you take. (While I've not found any one such facility providing *all* of these amenities, I have experienced each of those amenities at different clubs around the world). All of that really boils down to *hardware*: the services that we can purchase.

As group fitness instructors and personal trainers, however, we are the *software* that programs all of the hardware. Without us, the living, breathing, talented, qualified, entertaining, educational, and enriching aspect of the facility, the nuts and bolts are left to rust. We make it happen.

And so as we consider our topics of "education," "communication" and "cream," the purpose of this book comes to fruition: how great educators bring about independent changes in behavior in their students by a combination of both WHAT they do and HOW they do it on a world class level.

WHAT

WHAT: STABILITY AND MOBILITY
I oftentimes refer to the "S & M" of fitness. Truly, "stability and mobility" summarize my take on everything related to fitness, and in this order. It is NOT "M & S," because the stability concept precedes the mobility concept.

What do I teach in a class? First of all, I train both stability and mobility. I believe that, not only are these two concepts  interconnected, but that these two words summarize most components of fitness. "Stability" stands not only for strength and endurance, but also for proprioception, balance, kinesthetic awareness, and control. Arnold Schwarzennerger and Oprah Winfrey illustrate the concept of "stability." "Mobility" stands not only for movement, but also for flexibility, agility, coordination, and choreography. Imagine a baby involved in stabilizing on two legs and you will understand stability. Jackie Chan and Jim Carey illustrate the concept of "mobility." Imagine a baby happily exploring everything and you will understand mobility. These two concepts of fitness summarize our strengths are our weaknesses. Usually, we gravitate towards topics that emphasize our strengths. Almost all classes train both stability and mobility to some degree, but emphasize one. A stretch class, for example, emphasizes more muscular flexibility lengthening (mobility), whereas a body sculpting class emphasizes more strength (stability).

Which is your strength, stability or mobility? Where is the strength of your clients? When you train them, do you address both stability and mobility in all aspects of fitness? If you do not train both stability and mobility, do you at least recommend that clients train what they are NOT getting with you as they continue to train? For example, if a client only takes your body sculpting class (stability), do you recommend in-depth stretching or yoga (mobility)? If a personal training client only wants to work on agility drills (mobility), do you recommend balance and isometric training (stability)?

Cream trainers are always aware of the concepts of stability and mobility, and creatively manipulate them into training. Lisa Wheeler is perhaps the most talented hero of our industry. She is National Creative Manager for Equinox Group Fitness, Assistant Director and Choreographer for Fit Vid Productions, Contributing Editor for Shape Magazine, Associate Artistic Director for Ben Munisteri Dance Projects in New York City, fitness model, and an internationally acclaimed presenter and author. For years, hers was the name behind much of the content and editing of many of the Reebok University programs we know and love today. Lisa not only weaves the concepts of stability and mobility into her introductions, but she continues that theme throughout her experiences by developing ways to train both. In her famous "Lift, Leap, and Lunge," experience, during strength-enhancing movement series involving lunging/running (mobility), for example, she interjects balance tasks to train stability. Even if she is teaching dance (mobility), she incorporates a symmetrical eight-count move involving balance on each side. For example, she may teach a grapevine to the right (four counts), pulling up the left knee on the last count to make a balance option for another four counts training mobility and stability in one eight-count move!

I start with TWO interconnected premises involving a triangle. First, all experiences are designed to affect, usually to train, the individual, and this individual is made up of mind (brain), body (the muscles, ligaments, tendons, and organs that we train), and spirit (from Latin "spiritos," meaning "breath"). Second, in our movement experiences, we usually address one or more sections of a different triangle, made up of the three points representing our daily needs of cardiovascular, strength, and flexibility work. Connecting these two different triangles is my personal philosophy, which involves a related dichotomy of the terms "stability" and "mobility." To conceptualize this, the following may assist:

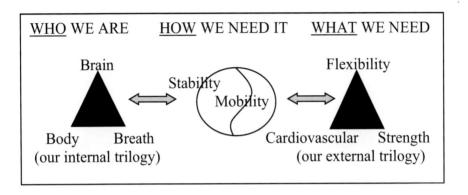

WHO WE ARE   HOW WE NEED IT   WHAT WE NEED

Brain

Stability

Mobility

Flexibility

Body   Breath
(our internal trilogy)

Cardiovascular   Strength
(our external trilogy)

Please notice that the left diagram depicts who we are in our core. On the far right appears what we need to best maintain a healthy approach to life. The center yin/yang symbol and the words "stability" and "mobility" serve as metaphors (with longer explanations elsewhere in this book) for understanding both triangles. These words of "stability" and "mobility" can help us understand what we are in the trilogy of our constitution (on the left), and they can also help us get a grasp on various efficacious ways to train the trilogy of our needs (on the right).

WHAT: WHAT ELSE DO WE TRAIN?
In starting a section of the book dedicated to "WHAT" I teach, perhaps the most important aspect of delineating the

17

"nuts and bolts" of movement has to do with the fact that I specifically try not to teach classes. If you pop a DVD into a player, that instructor on the screen is indeed your teacher, and leads you through exercises. I've always thought that there has to be MORE available to me when we have the opportunity of a LIVE class, so instead of saying "training a client" or "teaching a class," I prefer to "create an experience." How do you "create an experience" when you are just teaching choreography? This comes from both setting a theme for the experience and from carefully preparing the movements in class with attention to the five senses.

Even if I teach the same choreography to guests from week to week, the theme itself can change, and therefore drastically alter an experience. For example, following is a selection of the most popular of the themes I have set in different types of mind-body and traditional experiences over the years: "a focus on balance," "a focus on breathing," "your personal best today," "gently pushing yourself a bit harder today," "finding some element of home in every posture," "a soul biopsy," "partner work," "lighten up and laugh," and "concentration before activation." During the experience, I try to weave the theme into as many different aspects of the movements so that everyone continuously focuses on the theme.

WHAT'S IN A NAME

I may surprise you in a section discussing WHAT I train when I refrain from giving specific names of muscles, for example. From my observations of personal coaches and group fitness leaders around the world, I have seen an efficient trend over the years to empower people for daily life activities over training for training's sake. Truly, any section that explains WHAT I train *cannot* list a chain of muscles like "pyrimidalis," "biceps," and "transverses abdominus," for example, even though you may wish to find such specifics here. Instead, I subscribe to the philosophy to first study a client or an entire class and then create an experience that trains *movements*, not muscles, to emphasize *function* over physique.

Although this is a departure from the norm for many consumers and fitness professionals, I appeal to all those who teach movement in any form to think about their roles as movement specialists over other titles such as "personal trainers" or "group fitness leaders." Today with our expanded fitness roles in the industry, those of us who teach many disciplines and personal train many different types of clients (or do both!) are more "Movement Specialists" than any other title describes. I think that the title "aerobics instructor" is best left for the 1980's when that title was new. Similarly, "trainer" conjures up to me what men and women do in the circus with animals. I am thankful that most of us have evolved enough to call ourselves "fitness instructors" and "group fitness leaders" compared to those 1980 days. In the wet environment, however, this is not so. I still find the ubiquitous titles of "water aerobics teacher" in so many parts of the world. Just as we have evolved from those original "aerobics" titles on land, we also must reconsider expanding our aquatic titles to "aquatic fitness specialist," "group aquatic instructor," and even "aquatic movement lifestyle coach." Respect in the evolving industry of group and personal fitness coaching starts with the names we choose to call ourselves on all professionally printed matter like our business cards and group activity schedules.

SPECIFICS

When asking myself WHAT to train when preparing for a class or client, I use two steps. First, I begin by asking myself WHAT does the client do for a job? Knowing what types of actions a client is involved in on a daily basis tells us if that person needs more or less of certain actions. Whereas someone who stands all day working in an airport may need more spinal flexion to release constant extension, someone with a desk job hunched over a computer terminal for hours on end definitely has more need of extension to open up the anterior spaces in the vertebrae.

Second, when appropriate, I ask to look at my client's dress shoes to see how they wear. Sneakers don't show nearly the same kind of active foot patterns that more hard-toed shoes display. I like to know if my client has signs of supination, pronation, or even shows differences between sides. When I better understand the standing and walking habits based on posture and movement (stability and mobility) of my client, I can better decide WHAT to train.

When I do compile a program, I try to choose movements that do two things. First, I try to *enhance* life's movements. If a client needs upper body strength at work but possesses little in terms of strength and flexibility in that area, then I try to boost activities of daily life to enhance and ease what life requires. If someone works at UPS and needs to lift packages all day, I will work that client's upper body strength to enhance work and help prevent future suffering and injury. Second, I try to *balance* what is lacking by diminishing weakness in the weakest links of someone's kinetic chain. For example, for that same client who lifts packages at UPS, I would spend time stretching the hip flexors and muscles of the upper body to more muscular elongation to take care of muscles by helping to diminish muscle soreness. The questions to ask, therefore, are:

1. What does my client need more of to be able to do daily tasks more easily?

2. What is my client needing the MOST to promote self-care?

TRY THIS:

Try to answer the following, not for a client or a class, but for yourself first. You may bed at how long it takes you to decide on an answer, especially if you teach or train differently on different days.

1. In which actions do you need to be stronger on a daily basis? You can be general like stating "stability," but then try to be more precise. (For example, if you think you need more "stability" in your life, then specify "strength in xyz areas," "balance," etc).

_____
_____
_____
_____
_____
_____

2. Which actions do you need more of to promote your own self-care? You can be general like stating "stability," but then try to be more precise. (For example, if you think you need more "mobility," then specify "muscular flexibility," "more cardiovascular work," "more ability to get up and down easier," etc).

_____
_____

1 CORE AND 4 SYSTEMS

After those client considerations, I try to achieve both #1 and #2 for my clients and classes by 1. Training the core musculature before training the distal musculature, and by 2. incorporating all four muscular systems into my routines.

Much is said today about the "core" in "core training," and I like to invoke the NASM PT principles that describe the core as what passes through the hips or attaches to the spine, making virtually all musculature of the anterior, side, and posterior torso involved in the core. That said, we often overlook the root of the core; that is, sometimes we fail to have our clients and classes grasp that the most inner part of their core over which they have control is the pelvic floor first and the transversus abdominus second.

Notice the diagram of the muscles of the pelvic floor. Although there are physical internal and external differences between females and males in this area, both possess the major muscles of the pelvic floor seen in this diagram. I try to emphasize the importance of stability before mobility because I believe it precedes mobility. When we were young babies, we had to find stability on all fours before we learned the mobility skills to crawl everywhere. After that, we had to master stability on two legs before we learned the mobility skills to walk. Since stability begins at the core, and since the core begins with the pelvic floor, by syllogism, therefore, stability begins with the pelvic floor.

Much has been said of cueing this appropriately for classes and clients. Actually, the best way to cue it depends on demographics, age, conservativism, culture, and other issues. Generally, I use cues that depict body function, like "try to connect to the muscles that control elimination. This action makes you stronger, and is the start of your core."

The CORE Muscles: The Pelvic Floor

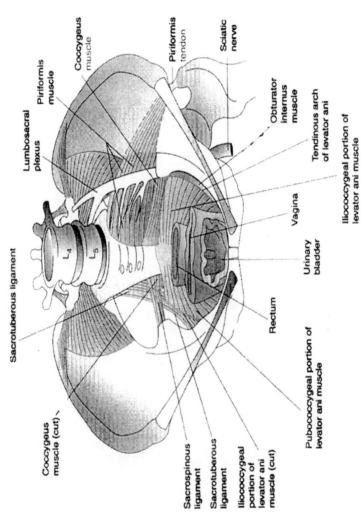

Coccygeus muscle (cut)

Sacrotuberous ligament

Lumbosacral plexus

Piriformis muscle

Coccygeus muscle

Piriformis tendon

Sciatic nerve

L4

L5

Sacrospinous ligament

Sacrotuberous ligament

Iliococcygeal portion of levator ani muscle (cut)

Pubococcygeal portion of levator ani muscle

Rectum

Urinary bladder

Vagina

Obturator internus muscle

Tendinous arch of levator ani

Iliococcygeal portion of levator ani muscle

FIGURE 19-7 Piriformis and pelvic area—superior view.

After contracting and closing the pelvic floor, the next part of the core that we can control is the transversus abdominus. The action of compressing the midsection brings about a greater stability and protection to the spine, decreases risk of injury, and can improve balance.

To summarize, I use my colleague Gin Miller's rhyme when I cue "activate the core; engage the pelvic floor." And my students know exactly what to do. And most of them smile.

While I can't put into words exactly WHAT I train with each client each time because both needs and people change, I can explain four things I always try to train. When compiling my ideas about WHAT exactly to train, I make sure that I train the four muscular pathway systems in the body. I find that when I think about the different ways to train these systems based on my clients' needs, I spend less time worrying about actual muscles worked and, consequently, provide a more rounded workout experience.

The four muscular systems I try to incorporate into every experience to create a well-rounded approach to training the internal and external trilogy are:
1. The Anterior Oblique System
2. The Posterior Oblique System
3. The Deep Lateral System
4. The Longitudinal System

The Anterior Oblique system respects the way the muscles run down the front of the body. If you stand with your arms overhead as I demonstrate on the right and visualize your muscles without skin, you'll notice that they run in a diagonal pattern. The very word "oblique" comes from the Latin meaning "diagonal." With the exception of the rectus abdominus fibers, all muscles down the front of the body run in a diagonal pattern. When we train in opposition, therefore, we train functional movement patterns exactly the way the muscles run to communicate with each other. An example of such an activity would be a standing left-leg single leg squat and right shoulder overhead press with a dumbbell.

Please notice how the muscles run in diagonal patterns down the front of the body:

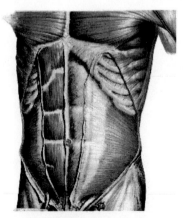

The Posterior Oblique system respects the way the muscles run down the back of the body. If you stand with your arms overhead as above and visualize your muscles without skin, you'll notice that they run in a diagonal pattern down the back of the body. With the exception of the erector spinae and multifidus fibers, all muscles down the back of the body run in a diagonal pattern. When we train in opposition, therefore, we train functional movement patterns exactly the way the muscles run to communicate with each other. An example of such an activity would be in an all four's position (called "quadruped" from the Latin root for "four") and doing opposite arm and leg reaches.

Please notice how the muscles run in diagonal patterns down the back of the body:

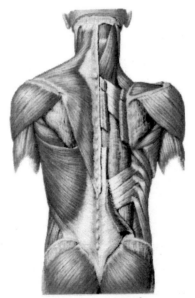

The Deep Lateral system respects the way the muscles run down the side of the body in such a way as to help side-bending. Many muscles assist in helping the body side-bend, but the true spinal lateral flexor is the quadratus lumborum. An example of training this system is doing spinal lateral flexion in a side-lying position, often called a "hip lift."

The Longitudinal system respects how the body keeps itself in various positions based on the pathway that muscles form down the same side of the body. Standing up requires two longitudinal systems working simultaneously, down the right and left sides of the body, respectively. An example of training this system is doing a left-leg single leg squat with an overhead press with the left shoulder. Notice how this differs from the Anterior Oblique system. When we train in opposition, we train oblique systems, and when we train same-side muscular patterns, we train the deep longitudinal system.

Just having to come up with exercises that train all four muscular systems in every experience helps us find the WHAT to train with our classes and clients because we exhaust the possibilities of training movements.

To be sure, this chapter cannot tell you exactly WHAT to train as a trainer or instructor. Even though some people may believe otherwise, I have solidified through the years my conviction that *movements are made for people, and not the other way around.* What I can be sure of in discussing WHAT I train is that, whatever the class or client program I develop, it supports my personal mission about what I believe in fitness.

MISSION & VISION STATEMENTS

I believe that all companies, organizations, clubs, facilities, and departments should have both mission and vision statements. A mission statement describes your personal philosophy about something as it stands today (in this case, work) and a vision statement is your personal desire of where you want it to move towards tomorrow. Over the years as a consultant, many clubs have invited me into their facilities to observe areas in which growth could attract more press, in which updates could occur, and in which training could make a difference. Before I agree to work with a facility, I always request that the facility emails me its personal mission statement. Perhaps you would be very surprised learning that only half of the facilities that invite me have mission and vision statements in place when they contract me!

Whether or not your facility and respective department has a mission statement, develop yours. Put it on the front or back of your business card, and refer to it often. Make sure if backs up everything you stand for in fitness. My mission statement as this book goes to print currently is: *"to orchestrate and coordinate balanced, mindful movement to make each client a champion of living."* My vision statement as this book goes to print is *"to do my part so that 'fitness' evolves into 'wellness' for more and more people whose quality of life could be improved on a daily basis beyond fitness facilities towards 'wellness without walls'."*

Your mission statement will help you determine WHAT it is that you train with every client and class. For example, notice the word "balanced" in my mission statement. When I work with a client, I emphasize different ways that the concept of balance affects daily life. This does not only refer to physical balance in all positions (standing, on all 4's, etc), but also in all aspects of our conceptual diagram outlined earlier: mental, spiritual, nutritional, cardiovascular, strength, and flexibility balance in many different ways. One way that I sought to introduce an innovative definition of balance began in the year 2000 when I decided to commence all group movement to the left instead of to the right, so from that date I began having my classes begin marching on the left, grapevining to the left, and stepping with the left.

When you have a personal mission statement that explains WHAT you are about, deciding WHAT to train with each client becomes so much easier. Both our mission and vision will continue to evolve in our changing business. I believe that we teach what we most need to learn and we learn what we most need to teach on a daily basis.

31

HOW

What separates the good from the great oftentimes is not WHAT instructors and trainers teach, but HOW. While I am sure that you will say that you do many of the suggestions in the rest of the book, I am not quite sure that any of us can claim with truth to do *all* of these. For example, effective strength training of the rectus abdominus without equipment involves a crunch: flexion in the sagittal plane in a supine position, driving the rib cage in the direction of the hips. When it's well taught,  a crunch is a crunch is a crunch. Most trainers can get individuals to initiate spinal flexion to train this muscle effectively and safely. The WHAT of the movement, the spinal flexion, is effective, but really not exciting in and of itself. What makes a truly excellent fitness leader, then, is the HOW he or she gets others to do the crunch, or any other form of movement.

POPULAR AND PROFESSIONAL

Many of us are popular instructors. People come to predict—and love—our style, and they return again and again to our classes because they like our product. For the lucky ones, there is standing room only in a profession where usually the numbers are important; club management is happy when there are lots of people in our classes because this signifies an effective experience for all.

Please consider a specific example. From a financial perspective, the more participants in a class, the better pricepoint for the budget per head. For example, if Mark has ten participants in her class and makes $50 per class, the cost per head to the club is $5. In other words, each student really is "costing" the club's budget $5. If she has twenty participants, however, the cost per head to the club reduces to $2.50. A popular cream instructor, however, while likely to make more money per class, is also likely to draw more participants. When cream instructor Lashaun teaches to fifty-five participants, even though she makes $100 per class, the cost per head to the club for that hour is a mere $1.80. Popularity, then, is justified both for educational and budgetary reasons.

Many of us are professional instructors. We teach according to our certifications' standards and guidelines, and use appropriate language and dress. A firm commitment not to stray from those guidelines regardless of creativity sets industry professionals apart from others.

Please consider another specific example. Many group instructors start out careers with the internationally-recognized, ubiquitous Primary Certification from AFAA. We add it to our list of certifications and seek employment. However, after about a year, it seems that we search for creativity in our classes, and sometimes this creativity comes at the expense of AFAA's Basic Exercise Standards and Guidelines (BESG). In the first few minutes of our classes, if we:

- side-chassé,
- rotate the spine,
- engage in high impact moves in the frontal plane (side to side),
- neglect to dynamically stretch the erector spinae muscle group,

or, if we do any of the following at *any* time during our classes:

- jump on one leg for more than 8 times, do more than 5 consecutive repeaters
- in step training,
- include only outdated static stretches in the warm-up

we are NOT teaching within the AFAA BESG! The goal of cream instructors is to fuse a high amount of creativity with a high amount of professionalism in being faithful at all times to industry guidelines.

Many of us know instructors and trainers who are either popular or professional, but not both. Some popular instructors teach to "packed" classes, but unfortunately may be teaching outdated, unsafe exercises that have gone unchanged for decades. Alternatively, some popular trainers may possess every major certification out there and look amazing on paper, but can't cue themselves out of a paper bag or build a popular client base.

Cream instructors are both popular *and* professional, and let's make this be our goal as we consider the suggestions throughout the rest of this book.

LESSONS AND THEMES

I said at the start of the book that an average trainer teaches a session or class, but an outstanding educator creates an experience. Truly, when that person is in charge, there is the feeling of a Broadway-like or Hollywood experience taking place because, like Donald Trump says, *everything* matters. All aspects of an experience come together to create that experience, and it usually starts with a theme. Great educators realize their roles as teachers, and refer to the fruits of their labor not as "classes," but "lessons." In each lesson, they begin with a theme, a central focus point that they want their students to maintain and see as a thread weaving through that day's lesson. Dr. Len Kravitz, Associate Professor at the University of New Mexico in Albuquerque, lectures using Microsoft PowerPoint® every day with his students in New Mexico. At the onset of each lecture, he always sets a theme on which he wants his students to focus. When I stand before a group of people and create an experience, I try to set a theme to emphasize a particular aspect of our time together. A theme could be any aspect of your experience that you single out at the onset for your participants. Following are a few different common themes I use regularly, and you'll notice that they could almost apply to every type of group experience or personal training session out there:

- "...today I invite you to focus on your breathing to make it sometimes a conscious activity. Instead of having to catch your breath, if you keep a focus on your breath you'll never lose it..."
- "...today's theme is 'my personal best,' so try to push yourself to give yourself exactly what you need today
- "...the theme for today's class is love. If you love what you do, then every push, every pull, and twist takes on a new meaning..."
- "...try to think about slowing down in today's class. Our theme is to reduce stress and improve concentration."
- "...today's theme is home. You'll notice that every song has to do with that, and my question to you will be in every position you are in 'If this is home, how does home feel now?'..."

Thinking of the type of classes you teach, the type of trainer you are, or both, add to the above list with a few themes that would be comfortable for you to say at the onset of your sessions:

_____

_____

_____

_____

_____

_____

_____

_____

_____

_____

_____

_____

_____

The next time you have a personal training client or teach a class, try setting a theme. Just think of something you want to emphasize and then think of three ways in which you can weave it into the experience you create, in your words or in the music. Maybe it's just inviting someone to think of life in terms of the triangles listed above and ask: "How am I facilitating the training of my internal trilogy in this experience?" If the breath itself is a theme of a particular class, I may choose to use one or more songs that emphasize that, like Faith Hill's "Just Breathe," for example. Creating music playlists around a theme are easy these days by just plugging in keywords to the Search engine built into Apple's own iTunes software.

Setting a theme is not mandatory, of course, but it is one way in which outstanding leaders set themselves apart from others. They make participants responsible for learning something, and assist that by giving a general assignment of focus by way of a theme.

CREATING EXPERIENCES

After they set a theme, great educators continue to create experiences inside and outside of their classrooms. You create an experience by: 1. Initiating true innovation into your craft, and by 2. trying to incorporate as much of the five senses as possible and as appropriate, each time.

Consider Sara Kooperman (scwfitness.com), president and CEO of SCW Fitness, based in Chicago. Among the many amazing business hats she wears, she both teaches regular classes and appears in over fifty internationally-selling DVDs. If you purchase a DVD of her "360° Yoga," for example, you observe an amazing class taught to participants whom invites to move around constantly, revolving their postures so that there ultimately is no front and back of the room. Her style is innovative, her tone professional and commanding, and interaction friendly.

This is the first definition of "creating an experience" because she truly displays innovation, going beyond what the competition does in innovation. If you actually take a class taught by Sara Kooperman, you will have a completely different experience, but an experience just the same. She demonstrates the second technique of creating an experience by invoking many different senses into the class. She touches (and even massages shoulders) during and at the end, (sense of touching), uses aromatherapy balm (sense of smelling), plays different styles of music (sense of hearing), entertains people with a friendly and humorous approach (sense of hearing), and has the class revolve so they are always changing their focus (sense of seeing).

Steve Feinberg of speedballfitness.com truly creates a show when he teaches. The classroom becomes a stage when he sings his cues, changes the lighting every ten minutes to create a different feel for each section of class, and personally connects with each person by learning names, singing cues, and making eye contact. He draws a crowd because he combines a theatrical, popular style with effective, professional programming.

How do you create an experience in every class or personal training session? To be sure, innovation is part of our very job description because we try to stay abreast of new techniques and trends. Becoming familiar and comfortable with different ways to incorporate the five senses into training is often unexplored. Following are a few ideas to get you thinking about changing up the way you incorporate sense-ual training.

To entertain the senses, consider the following suggestions incorporating the five senses:

HEARING
MUSIC: I try to choose music that compliments the experience at hand in a *thematic* nature; whatever the particular theme of a class could be, I try to emphasize that with music. Above all, I try to choose either silence or music consciously so that it adds to, rather than detracts from, the overall experience.

When a smooth experience is the goal, remember to push the "continuous" feature on the CD or iPod so that, when a particular CD or playlist finishes before your movement, the playlist starts again from the beginning. If you do not do that, you have to leave your  place, go to the sound system, make adjustments, and return to your area to teach. If, in fact you do use an iPod, I

40

recommend purchasing a small remote control for it so that you can navigate volume and track selection from virtually anywhere in your room. This is particularly helpful for yoga and cycling playlists where not all songs play at the same volume and we can instantly raise or lower the sound appropriately without having to leave our spot. I keep my little remote control always in my pocket or tucked into my waistline and have instant control to volume at any time of my experience.

VERBAL CUEING: Do you make yourself cue the same thing with different words? You may be surprised how creatively you may develop phrasing to say the same thing in an innovative way, and, what's more, your participants usually pay more focus on newer phraseology.

TRY THIS:

How would you cue if you eliminated the following phrases from your vocabulary for a time? How many different ways can you think of to say the following *without* using the following words?

1. "engage your abs"	
2. "beginner, intermediate, advanced"	
3. "don't hold your breath"	
4. "keep your spine straight"	
5. "go!"	
6. "contract your pelvic floor"	
7. "show me good posture"	
8. "shoulders back and down"	
9. "squeeze"	
10. "Come on!" "Turn it up!"	

While the chart shows not only my least favorite cues, I find that it shows cues that become non-specific to our participants and they really end up hearing what sounds like Charlie Brown's teacher whose words actually are unintelligible. I will discuss more in the LANGUAGE section. (At the end of the book appears the same chart with some creative suggestions in case you get stuck...but I URGE you to try to fill in this section without peeking first.

Perhaps the most important tip regarding HEARING comes in the thought that, in every personal or group session, there is always one person who cannot see. For this person hinging on every single verbal cue that you make, precision, accuracy, motivation, and energy level are key.

TRY THIS:

Picture a movement series or exercise from the last session or class you instructed. Now, imagine someone in front of you who is either blindfolded or blind, and cue the same movement series or exercise to someone who cannot see your demonstrations or facial expressions. Offer corrections and tips that are precise and specific so that the "blind" person can understand what you intend from your words. Try to offer instructional cues that affect safety, alignment, execution, motivation, and modifications, with a keen sense of specificity to words. Remember our definition of "communication" as "the response you get regardless of your intent," because you will definitely learn immediately how good of a verbal cuer you are based on what you see. The instructor with excellent verbal cueing skills will profit in situations where the lights go off, for example, or when everyone is in a yoga posture without visual access to the teacher, yet everyone follows precise verbal cueing.

When you offer feedback, instead of saying "good," offer more specifically WHAT merits an accolade. For example, "Your posture is perfect, Sherry," or "I like the way you are exhaling forcefully on the effort, Alex," are examples of specific positive feedback.

Shannon Fable (sfresources.com), recipient of the 2006 ACE Instructor of the Year award, Consultant, Presenter and Owner of Sunshine Fitness Resources, says "my biggest pet peeve is unnecessary cueing. There are MANY forms of unnecessary cueing, but the top culprits are constantly counting backwards from 8 (pretty sure they know how to do that!), 'up for 2 and down for 2' (do they really care?) and filler motivation or ambiguous language such as: 'good job', 'you got it', 'that's it' (got what? what did I do good?). It's an easy fix ... *cue when necessary and make it specific.* Many times instructors say so much for fear of dead airspace that their brilliance is lost in the shuffle. Learning to be critical about cue choices, enunciating key points and providing silence so participants can get the message is crucial to the success of your group."

Excellent verbal cueing skills help make a cream instructor, and we will explore more about choosing effective words later on.

SMELLING

AROMATHERAPY: I try to choose aromatherapy when appropriate. With the go-green movements on the planet, lighting smoking incense is not the most environmentally-conscious way to make a room smell great. Instead, I create an inexpensive aromatherapy spray that works well when sprayed on the skin and also when sprayed into the room before guests arrive. Sometimes I spray the room before guests arrive, and sometimes I allow participants to spray themselves before class, and still at other times I will spray participants when they finish in the supine position on the floor, like after yoga, for example. Of course, before I walk around and spray an entire room in "corpse posture," I always announce what I will do and invite those not wishing to get a gentle spritz of warm aromatherapy spray to cover their faces with a towel or other item of clothing. The recipe for what I put in my aromatherapy spray is found at www.findlawrence.com under FREE STUFF for FITNESS TIPS.

TASTING

IN: When appropriate, I try to incorporate taste into my experience in two ways. First, I think that great instructors should put experiences together in good taste, which means using inclusive language, avoiding offensive and non politically-correct terminology, and cueing with a lot of positive feedback.

IN FOOD: During a seated posture in yoga, for example, I may offer candies flavored with natural mint, which complements the aromatherapy spray of the same flavor, which, in turn, could complement a theme of "cooling breath."

SEEING

CLOTHES: Dressing the professional part is paramount to creating a key experience. Some industry leaders take extra steps to make the visual sight a well-planned experience. Lyndsay Murray-Kashoid based in Dallas, Texas, for example, color coordinates her eyeshade and pedicure with the color of the yoga mat she will use on a particular day. Dr. Len Kravitz always wears a flashy, multi-colored shirt purchased from among his favorite shops in Las Vegas to make impact, and in fact refers to these shirts as his "impact shirts from Vegas." Deborah Puskarich, Group

Movement Coordinator for Dr. Cooper's Craig Ranch facility, coordinates coloring among her clothes (from caps to clothes to shoes) including matching these colors to the colors used in any equipment in that class. Kayoko Takada of Athlie Sports Clubs in Tokyo, Japan, gives herself a weekly manicure, pedicure, daily blow-dry, and hourly make-up touch-up between classes to stay on top of the Japanese attention to detail in taking great pride in presenting appearance. I try to establish a traditional connection between traditional color and my clothes, so that I will incorporate something in white for yoga, in black for T'ai Chi, in red for core conditioning, etc..

LIGHTING: On Broadway, it's often said that lighting can make or break a show. A musical can be just horrible, but if the lighting is exemplary, everyone at least looks flawless at all times. Similarly, lighting in a gym or studio can flatter, set the mood, heighten an experience, de-stress, motivate, and even empower. Being able to change the lighting often may prove distracting, but great instructors not only match lighting to the mood of an experience, but match the lighting to the mood *continuously*. For example, if a certain section of a class finds people supine staring into fluorescent lights, the instructor will modify that to make the experience more pleasant for SIGHT. Similarly, WHAT is illuminated can be just as important as HOW something is illuminated. When I began coordinating classes for the Golden Door Spa in Puerto Rico, I realized that there was a great deal of time when participants were on their backs facing the fluorescent lights and the dry, white ceiling. I was told that there was no budget to change this, so I went to a local discount store and purchased light blue paint, blended it with white paint from the Engineering department, took a sponge from my kitchen, and painted light clouds across the ceiling of our movement studio. This gave guests something more appealing for their SIGHT when supine than a fluorescently-lit white-boarded ceiling.

VISUALIZATION

If you are thinking that there's little you can do in terms of what your participants see because you have little or no control over your actual area, think again. The power of visualization is sometimes more powerful than actually what you see. Why do we sometimes close our eyes in stressful situations? We do this because we know that we can create inside a more beautiful place, if only for a moment. When we teach people the power of visualization, we make our roles as educators bigger, transcending fitness towards wellness. When we show people how to draw on their own, internal power, we show them that they can always use their internal sense of sight to change what they see. Helen Vanderburg, Olympian athlete and recipient of the 2005 IDEA Group Fitness Instructor of the Year

Award, says, "if you change the way you see things, the thing you see will change."

TRY THIS:

Picture a movement series or exercise from the last session or class you instructed. Now, imagine someone in front of you cannot hear, or who is from a country whose language you do not speak so that any words you utter are unintelligible. Now, teach the same movement series or exercise to someone who cannot depend on your words, but only on your expressions, gestures, and visual cues. Try to offer instructional cues that affect safety, alignment, execution, motivation, and modifications, all without words. Offer corrections and tips that are precise and specific so that the "deaf" person can understand what you intend from your body language alone. Remember our definition of "communication" as "the response you get regardless of your intent," because you will definitely learn immediately how good of a visual cuer you are based on what you see. The instructor with excellent visual communication skills will perform well under pressure with audio-visual mishaps, such as a missing microphone, for example, or will be able to reach those in class who do not command the same language as the instructor.

Perhaps the most important tip regarding SEEING comes in the thought that, in every personal or group session, there is always one person who cannot hear. For this person hinging on every single visual cue that you make, precision, accuracy, motivation, and energy level are key.

Two of the world's greatest visual cuers are Calvin Wiley (calvinwiley.com) and Tony Stone (tonstone@aol.com). As international choreographers, Calvin and Tony travel to many countries where they do not speak the local language, yet after a simple "hello" in English, they proceed to get thousands able to move to music, without verbal instruction. Truly, they do not even require a microphone. Honed are their skills of visual cueing. With facial expressions and gesticulations, they are able to move a room of thousands with no words.

In creating an experience, then, I invite you to ask yourself how *complete* of a sensual cuer you are; that is, how well do you incorporate ALL of the aforementioned senses when you instruct? Do you say "grapevine right" (verbal cueing, great for the blind person and verbal learner) or do you just point to the right (visual cueing, great for the deaf person and the visual learner), or do you both speak *and* point (optimal).

Excellent visual cueing skills help make a cream instructor.

TOUCHING
EMOTIONAL: Touching clients and classes in an emotional way is something

that cream instructors have learned to do. When you teach something physical, you affect the body, but when you teach something physical with attention to the trilogy of the brain and breath, training becomes emotional. Petra Kolber (petrakolber.com), recipient of the 2001 IDEA International Instructor of the Year award, continuously filters emotional stories into her sessions. Whether it's about overcoming Hodgkin's Lymphoma in New York City, seeing a Cirque du Soleil production in Las Vegas, or visiting Bali with her sister for the first time, Petra always brings an emotional, touching story to every experience she creates. When you touch the heart of your class in addition to touching their body, you help them remember the good feeling they get when they "experience" you, and that is good job security.

One of history's greatest teachers was Jesus Christ. A common thread that unites all of his teaching techniques is the thread of comment he made when claiming "I am the way, the truth, and the light." On close inspection, his teachings relate to the senses we have been examining. Jesus rarely taught anyone to do something by giving commands; instead, he taught in metaphors and parables. All of his teaching parables deal with something having to do with the "way," the "truth," or "light." The "way" stories really have to do with the sense of direction regarding the sense of sound. The "truth" stories relate to the sense of feeling.

51

The "light" stories relate to the stories of sight. Sometimes when we teach, while we cannot speak in parables, philosophical, Jesus or Buddha-like statements can leave our guests thinking more of their lives beyond fitness. For example, if it's a part of your style and if you feel comfortable with the suggestion, just a prepared quote you memorize and say at an appropriate time could influence your students in a positive way beyond the bicep. For example, sometimes I quote the Bible when I say "If you want what you've never had, you have to do what you've never done," and "It's important to worry about what goes *into* the heart, but it's even more important to worry about what comes *out* of the heart" (Samuel).

TRY THIS:

I invite you to take a moment to write down 5 unique things about yourself that have nothing directly related to fitness that are not dire secrets. For example, two unique things about me that not many people know are 1. I love to cook, especially with dark chocolate, and 2. I like to watch the ABC Daytime soap opera "General Hospital." List here some of your lesser-known likes or favorite things to do or famous people you've met:

1._____

2. _____

3. _____

4. _____

5. _____

Now, here's the challenge, try to incorporate just one of those unique pieces of yourself. Over time, you'll become more familiar with interjecting a personal story—however short—into your sessions, and you will be surprised how your participants will react to you because you are touching them on an emotional level. Jay Blahnik (jayblahnik.com), recipient of the 1996 IDEA Instructor of the Year and 2006 Can Fit Pro Instructor of the Year award, consistently blends an ideal amount of personal anecdote into both the theoretical and practical sections of his classes. His impeccable ability to let participants get to know him while he educates them keeps them coming back for more. In future, I invite you to return to the above list and choose 5 more lesser-known facts about yourself that maybe are more personal, such as a medical incident, a story about your childhood, or somewhere you lived before you moved to the current location. Relax about wondering exactly *where* to insert your personal stories; the moments will present themselves.

PHYSICAL: Physical touching in the fitness industry can be a controversial topic in the United States. In most overseas countries, touching clients is either allowed, or not even discussed by law. In the litigious US, however, there are some states where touching clients is either not allowed or done with caution. Be that as it may, I always find hugs appropriate after class. During class, as I walk by participants, I try to touch them by making long-lasting eye contact and remembering their name. That alone can touch a person who otherwise will have a stress-ridden day! If I know that it's okay to touch someone physically, I will always do so in plain view of others, and always above the heart level, such as touching a shoulder as I walk by someone and offer specific, positive feedback, like "Your posture is really tall, Connie; good for you." I know that, if it would not be for us, there are some people who take our classes who otherwise would not be touched at all.

CORRECTIONS: I have learned from teaching large groups that oftentimes the best way to make a correction to an individual student is a verbal one. Try to make a general statement, like "be sure to keep your shoulders down while you are cycling." If someone still does not make a change in behavior, then using that person's specific name (or other specific characteristic) is necessary. For example, "Ankie, try to lower your shoulders," or "Hello my friend in the white shirt in the back with the great smile, try to keep your shoulders down, and keep up the great smiling!" If you have to single someone out for safety, try to sandwich that corrective cue between two positive feedback statements. Alternatively, if you can leave your place, perhaps turning off the microphone and whispering a specific cue directly to Ankie may also be appropriate.

One of the most kinesthetically-aware techniques I use as a personal and group trainer draws on touch, but in reverse. Instead of touching a client, I invite the client to touch me. For example, imagine Lisa in a yoga class with a really unsafe downward-facing dog (pike) posture. She is looking up to the sky, her knees are pointing in different directions, her ribs are digging into her pelvis, and one heel is off the floor while another is pressing into it. If it's appropriate for me to leave my place and go to her, I would kneel beside her and try to correct the aforementioned issues one-by-one, saying: *"Lisa, I am putting my hand under your chin; can you tuck your chin towards my hand until you touch me so that your neck alignment improves? Now, I am putting my hands behind your knees; can you push the backs of your knees into my hands so that your legs get longer and more symmetrical? Now I am putting my hand a bit higher than your glutes; can you push up your buttocks towards my hand to lengthen your spine? Finally, I am putting my hands under both of your heels; try to push your heels down into my fingers to feel your hamstrings lengthen."*

Notice how I never touch Lisa: I cue so that *she* has to touch *me*. Instead of spending time emphasizing any *problem*, I put my hands toward the *solution* and make her responsible for moving towards it. When

I choose words, I try to incorporate the *purpose* in each movement. Ultimately, I make Lisa responsible for her own corrections because, first, she has to understand my cues around her body, and second, she has to take responsibility towards the solution of each body area, with an understanding of *why*.

TRY THIS:

Have a friend or relative stand in front of you and slouch. Invite him or her to stand with lopsided knees, pelvis, shoulders, and head. Use the "touching technique" to bring about better posture. Put your hand towards the solution and invite your friend to move towards it for each section of the body that needs attention. You may wish to put your hand towards where you want a bodypart to move and cue "touch my hand here with your head," for example.

Creating an experience means being an innovator at your incorporation of the six senses. I always find it difficult when someone says "just define your style." It is no easy task. Instead, it is a lifelong process. My hope is that the ideas in this book serve to help you say "this could or could not be part of my style." This book just serves to offer a collection of options. No one's style should match every person's style, but just being aware of how other great teachers incorporate the six senses into education can help stimulate your own innovative process.

OPENINGS AND EXITS:
THE FIRST 5 AND THE LAST 5

Petra Kolber of group exercise fame knows the importance of an opening and closing. "People will always remember the first five minutes and the last five minutes," she says, "so it's really important to prepare those sections of a class. You may have a train wreck in the middle, but people will take away how they feel at the beginning and the end." To be sure, most people come to our experiences ready to move immediately and do not want to listen to a long introduction. Nevertheless, I have always found that a formal introduction—regardless of personal style inside of the experience—can set a tone for professionalism.

GROUP FITNESS

To create an amazing opening for group fitness, I try to begin with an official, formal opening. I choose the word "Namaste," from Sanskrit because it is one of the oldest, if not *the* oldest, greeting on the planet. It denotes both "hello" and "goodbye," like "aloha" in Hawaiian, "ciao" in Italian, "shalom" in Hebrew, and "giassu" in Greek, but it also connotes "my inner peace meets, greets, and salutes the light in you." Regardless of the country or language preference, I always begin punctually with this word, followed by the exact name of the experience. I then express gratitude to people for attending, because I see myself as the host of a party and, if you come to a party of mine, the first thing I would say is "lovely to see you; how sweet of you to come." After that, I establish the purpose of the experience so that everyone knows what to expect. This is important so that everyone knows under what cognitive framework you are working. People will always judge, but if you establish your purpose before commencing, you give people the time to decide if an experience will be right for them.

For example, let us consider that you are teaching a class called "Power Yoga," and you have prepared a few asana to be held for long durations of time. Let us also consider that there are students coming to the experience because they have taken a class with the same name elsewhere, and expect a similar class format based on their previous experience. At the outset, if you define what "power yoga" means to you as a basis for the ensuing format you are about to teach, you allow them to decide if they want to stay or leave. If they do stay and find that they enjoyed a different approach to power yoga, then everyone is happy. If they do stay and do find that they do not enjoy your interpretation of power yoga (at least on this day), then two things have happened. First, you have allowed them to learn something about yoga that they otherwise may never have experience, and know that, henceforth, they are more comfortable with a very specific type of yoga approach. Second, if they analyze your style after class, they cannot fault your format because you have introduced *your* purpose at the start of the experience. I oftentimes use the metaphor of travel at the start of an experience with my students and personal training clients: "I am your (mind-body) travel guide today, and today the journey I'm going to invite you to go on with me will explore ...(insert here your class purpose)..."

I also try to include in the class introduction a mention about the equipment we will use, a mention suggesting how to measure intensity, a reminder that I will be offering modifications, which means teaching *regressions* (ways to make movements easier) and *progressions* (ways to make movements more challenging) for some movements along the way. I acknowledge that movements are made for people and not the other way around, so I say "if a movement does not seem right for you, it's probably not, so remember that learning to listen to your body is also part of fitness and wellness." If there is any research that supports what we will be doing, I either include it now or introduce it in bits during the experience. Finally, because I have found since starting in 1983 that oftentimes individuals come into class very serious-- from the expressions on their faces to their attitudes about fitness in general (especially in New York City)--I remind them that "one of my goals is to entertain the inner child, so it is okay to smile, if only on the inside at the start. I believe it is more important to be serious *about* work, but not serious *at* work. I used to be really serious, too, and learned young in life that "serious" gives you ulcers. I also learned to lighten up because "the reason that angels can fly is that they take themselves so lightly." Usually after that most people smile, and those who refuse have at least stopped frowning and uncrossed their arms.

    Because the introduction of every class or session is so paramount to creating an effective experience, here are some other tips from world-class presenters and personal trainers that may assist you in developing your own "entrance" and "exit" style.

- Mindy Mylrea (mindymylrea.com), recipient of the 2004 Can Fit Pro International Presenter of the Year and of the1999 International IDEA Fitness Instructor of the Year awards, always gets her participants to laugh in the first five minutes of her sessions. This is a perfect ice-breaker to lower stress and raise the feeling of camaraderie.
- Maureen Hagan, PT, vice president of operations for GoodLife Fitness in Canada and recipient of the 2006 IDEA Fitness Instructor of the Year award, always tells you at the

start of a session exactly "what you are going to get." This builds up your expectations and builds up even more excitement for the upcoming session.

- Keli Roberts (keliroberts.com), recipient of the 2003 IDEA International Instructor of the Year award, always starts a session by revealing the new research that supports it. She takes sometimes complicated research information, converts it to simple vernacular, and makes it sound so exciting with her blend of theory into practical demonstration.

Now that we have discussed the importance of openings, we have to back track for a moment. The actual class or personal training session does not always begin at the clock time. Truly, most successful experiences include a "pre-show." If you have ever attended a performance by Cirque du Soleil, you will recall that, before the show's official opening, clowns or other actors from the show mingle with the crowd as early as twenty minutes before the official start time. The preshow builds excitement, diminishes traditional barriers between the audience and actors, and changes the expectations of participants so they know that not all action will occur strictly on the stage, but around them.

While a preshow may be difficult for personal trainers and group fitness instructors with busy schedules today, sometimes it is possible. A preshow can mean:

- Chatting with guests outside of the studio while waiting for a current class to finish
- Walking around a room to greet clients personally and learn their names
- Bring something reminiscent of childhood school years to "show and tell" to the students, like an aromatherapy spray, hand sanitizer, candy or similar treat, or simply something from your personal life you want to share. I remember when the first Pepperidge Farms® Mint Milano cookies came out I was so impressed that I had to take a bag to my class. When Electrasol Dishwashing Powerball Tabs first came out, I took one to my Monday morning ladies where I was teaching at the time in Dallas, Texas, and showed them something that was going to change their kitchen lives forever.   Ultimately, you achieve many of the same results that Cirque du Soleil achieves in the preceding paragraph, with little effort.

Taking the time to create an experience before the actual official time lets the guests know how much you value them because you are starting your "job" even before you have to. I have witnessed too many instructors standing by their stereo controls waiting for the official class time to register on the clock while ignoring a room full of participants and the importance of showing how much you care. At the end of the day, people do not care about how much you really know, but they do need to *feel* how much you *care*.

PERSONAL TRAINING

The first five minutes of a personal training session are just as important as the first five minutes of a group experience. Todd Durkin (toddurkin.com), winner of the 2004 IDEA and 2005 ACE Personal Trainer of the Year awards, uses the start of a personal training session to set the theme, to gain confidence, and to guide. Todd and his team create award-winning personal training experiences daily, and share some of their secrets here:

Begin with a 5 minute general warm-up that could be an easy jog, power walk, skipping rope, or work on an elliptical trainer, bike, or any other machine. This should be immediately followed by a 5-10 minute dynamic warm-up. The purpose of the dynamic warm-up is to activate the neuro-muscular system from feet to fingertips, warm-

*up the fascia, and prepare the body
for the activity that is about to occur.
Examples of the dynamic warm-up
include jumping jacks, skipping,
bodyweight lunges, bodyweight
squats, inch-worms, and cariocas.
Use the dynamic warm-up as an
integral part of a workout as it will
decrease your chance for injury,
improve flexibility, and improve
overall preparedness for your
exercise session. Additionally, it will
help with coordination, movement
skills, and assist with reinforcing
proper mechanics.*

The closing of an experience is equally, if not more, important than the start. The closure is the time to restate the purpose, remind them of the theme of the experience, and show them that you truly have taught them something. Ultimately, the most successful word after safety in every experience is *success*, so this is the time to make that happen if it has not occurred previously so that everyone leaves on a positive note. At the end of a class in movement, lecture, or personal training session, I summarize what we set out to do, reminding them of the promises we made at the outset. When they realize that I did deliver exactly as promised, they appreciate our ability that much more. Todd Durkin finishes a personal training session with consistency. He says:

*After your session, it is very
important to finish with a post-
workout flexibility routine. This
routine should be for your entire body*

so that you can improve flexibility, help your recovery, and just feel good. Unlike the dynamic warm-up that emphasizes movement and integrated flexibility, the post-workout flexibility routine should emphasize more static exercises. Examples may include the downward facing dog, pigeon pose, lying hamstring stretch, kneeling hip flexor stretch, and a doorway chest/arm stretch. Post workout stretches can be held for 30-60 seconds or longer and deep breath work is encouraged during this time. Be sure to stretch at the end of your program and your body and mind will be very appreciative because these are the good feelings and endorphins that the clients will take away with them.

Douglas Brooks (MovesInFitness.com), Exercise Physiologist and a personal training mentor of mine, says that the ending reflects an opportunity to get to the emotional side of personal training. He says:

Oftentimes, trainers fail to recognize the value of building relationships and customer service people skills. Sometimes the focus shifts too much toward programming or introduction of the latest piece of equipment or teaching methodology. When this happens, the client and humanity of the relationship often takes a back seat. When the relationship is compromised, a personalized, service oriented business like personal training is more likely to struggle or fail. I like to close my sessions with a recap of the successes and accomplishments, clarifying what the

client would like to do better or
accomplish before, or during the next
session.

Furthermore, the end of a personal training session is also a time for selling. Sherri and Alex McMillan (nwpersonaltraining.com and nwwomensfitness.com), are internationally-recognized leaders in the world of personal training development, winning the 2006 IDEA Fitness Director(s) of the Year award, the 1998 IDEA Personal Trainer(s) of the Year award, and the1998 Can Fit Pro Presenter(s) of the Year award. This team has proven an in-depth understanding about developing personal training skills in this area of "closing" the last five minutes of a personal training session. They write:

As Fitness Professionals, most of us spend a
great deal of time and energy developing
our technical and practical skills. Yet, very
few of us have ever obtained any extensive
sales training. Bottom line – no matter what
you're doing, if you want to be successful
you have to learn how to sell yourself. Can
you imagine any successful corporation
running its organization without sales staff
and sales training? No, a leading-edge
company realizes the importance of its sales
staff and the need for extensive training in
sales no matter what it's selling.

But in our industry, most fitness
professionals are uncomfortable with the
any form of selling. You're in the fitness
industry not because you love selling but
because you love helping people. But you
need to sell to get people to experience your

services! Remember that selling is not a bad thing! We are selling a very good thing - improved health and fitness, more energy, enhanced confidence and self-esteem, and longevity. You must believe in yourself and your services!! Remember that if people have called you or inquired about your services, they are interested. They are just waiting for you to convince them that you can help them. And even if they haven't contacted you initially and you've approached them, everyone is our world can benefit from what we have to offer so don't be shy.

> *We have to be very up-front with you. If you are going to succeed as a fitness professional, you must become a top-notch salesperson. It will make no difference whether you hold all the highest credentials and certifications if you can't influence people to invest in your services or products. So, consider this, by developing your selling skills, not only will this enable you to generate a higher income, it will also allow you to help and impact more people's lives.*

Traditionally, we referred to the endings of our sessions as "cool downs." Given the evolving nature of the fitness industry, this has changed. Maureen Hagan's choice of the word "transitions" far better describes the last moments of our experiences. To "cool down" really means to prepare the body for rest, to leave it in a milder state, and ready for bed. Our clients, however, are far from cool down after class: they rush to take an additional class, to get showered, to daycare to pick up the children, to go to work. A "transition" better describes what happens at this time: we transition them from one level, set, and type of movement to another set of movement, referred to as their "life."

Cream rises when we are able to turn a class or session into the type of high school essay writing method we all learn: introduction, body, and conclusion. The conclusion, or "transition," actually guarantees our job security because it is only here that we use the opportunity to show the clients exactly how much we impact their life through fitness and wellness, and helps to leave them wanting more.

Whether I lecture using Powerpoint or teach a workshop with theory but without projection, my last two "slides" are always the same. First, I always do a summary by restating the purpose and revisiting the objectives I promised to deliver, just like in the high school essay we learned that the last paragraph should restate the first paragraph, using different words. Even if I have taught a Latin dance class, there is still a purpose to which we can return and summarize.

Second, I use the transition time to discuss four topics briefly:
1. Homework
   This means giving the participants something simple to do that transcends our class together.

Examples could be "Remember that breathing technique we learned today? I invite you to try it once before you go to bed before we meet again," or "We learned a new way to stabilize today and I want you to try it on your own sometime when you're not at the gym." When a trainer or instructor gives homework, it shows how important people are to him or her and, furthermore, helps close the gap between fitness and life, between the things the participants do and ponder when they are inside of the fitness environment versus away from it.

2. What's the take-home message? This is the summary of the session for someone who could not attend. Imagine that someone missed your class, pt session, or lecture, and asked you to summarize your message from that time period in one sentence. It is harder than you might think, so practicing a one-sentence take-home message for your participants before you actually do it in front of them will make it easier. When I miss someone's class or session, I always ask participants "what was the take-home message?" When participants can succinctly summarize the instructor's

experience in a sentence, I know that he or she was effective at letting participants know the purpose of the session. Do your participants walk away from each class or personal training session able to summarize in one sentence what you did together?

3. The transition is also a time for gratitude. Set yourself apart from the rest by thanking everyone who came to your experience personally, if possible. If you have a class of ten or more individuals, and if you teach those individuals regularly, you can express gratitude to each of them on a personal basis. If, however, your class is too large for that, or if you teach to different faces every day (such as in a day-spa environment), then you may consider using the "verbal hug" approach. For this to work, all you have to do is know the names of three individuals in your class from different parts of the room. By concluding class saying "I want to thank you for coming to this experience today; from Bernard on this side to Katrina in the back, all the way over to Irene on the left, I want to thank each of you for joining me," you are making a verbal hug of your participants, using words to make everyone feel

included. You are covering the entire room with your comments. The great part about this technique is that, while it is personal, you only have to know the names of 3 others in the class!

4. Cream instructors also use the transition time to plant a "teaser." This is when an instructor generates anticipation about the next experience by either demonstrating a fancy move that everyone will be learning next time (to instill that "I want to do THAT" feeling) or simply says "next time you will love it when we ...."

Becoming familiar with your own openings and closures can help you create valid lesson plans for your participants. Planned starts and endings prove to participants that you are prepared and polished. Knowing you have to deliver a clear-cut purpose and objectives will make you think carefully about the development of your experiences. Cream rises when you have a product so evolved that, regardless if it is movement, lecture, or personal training, the very nature of your own methodology becomes predictable, recognizable, and consistent, and to this consistency we now turn.

AND METHODOLOGY
Starbucks has been hugely successful on a global scale. The company strives to

offer a consistent product so that, from Memphis to Moscow, a Starbucks "venti sized coffee with cream to go" looks, feels, smells, and tastes the same the world over. Notice how many senses are involved in consistency in our Starbucks analogy: four out of five.

Similarly, when you teach and train, is your product consistent? Of course, your *style* changes based on mode, equipment, music, location, demographics of the participants, and even cultural influence, but are you still consistent in your method of product delivery? Do you incorporate the five senses in similar ways when you teach? Do you deliver a predictable, high-quality product regardless of the venue and technical or scheduling challenges?

Rob Glick, recipient of the 2006 Can Fit Pro International Presenter of the Year award, exemplifies how cream rises because he delivers a consistent product, despite occasional challenges with language, audio-visual, sound, stage, health, or equipment. Even with those issues, Rob never falters but instead continues to rise to the occasion to create an experience so that all participants feel successful. I have had the privilege of teaching at conventions where Rob also was guest teaching, in Russia, China, Italy, Turkey, the United Kingdom, and throughout the United States. When I have time off and want to attend a workout, I always take Rob's class because I know that, regardless of the type of class, he creates a similar experience with a consistent product. Rob Glick is my consistent "Starbucks" fitness fix.

I have been referencing the word "product" several times now in relation to fitness. Your total product is the total sum creation of experience. Delivering a product consistently comes from having a predictable methodology. If someone asked you what your methodology is for teaching, do you have a concrete answer? Or, do you just stand in front of clients and classes and "get it done" in any way that makes them follow you?

Cream instructors and trainers have a predictable method of delivering their product. Consider a strength or flexibility class. How do you get people to follow you? To be sure, you most probably rely on a combination of verbal and visual cues to bring about changes in behavior. What specifically is your system?

When analyzing any exercise, the Aerobics and Fitness Association of America have the AFAA 5 Questions™ for analyzing movement. These are:

1. What is the purpose of this exercise? (e.g., muscular strength or endurance, cardiorespiratory conditioning, flexibility, warm-up or activity preparation, skill development and/or stress reduction).

2. Are you doing that effectively? (e.g., proper range, speed or body position against gravity)

3. Does the exercise create any safety concerns? (e.g., potential stress areas, environmental concerns or movement control)

4. Can you maintain proper alignment and form for the duration of the exercise? (e.g., form, alignment or stabilization)

5. For whom is the exercise appropriate or inappropriate?

Those five questions inspired me to create, not only a method for evaluating movement, but also my own personal methodology. To be sure, the following does not have to be your own methodology of delivery when you instruct, but practicing using these steps can assist you in being sure that your own style is as complete as possible.

The following five steps I recommend as methodology for strength, flexibility, and, to a lesser degree, cardiovascular, instruction. Notice that they all begin with the same letter "p."

1. Purpose
2. Position ("stability")
3. Progression/Regression ("mobility")
4. Prana ("breath")
5. Extras: "Personal" (Transference, Humor, Interesting, Education, Feeling)

Imagine teaching someone standing in front of you holding dumbbells or cans of soup how to do a biceps curl effectively as you read an example of how to make the five steps above more practical. The quotation marks depict actual cues as if this were a script:

1. PURPOSE: "We're gonna do standing bilateral biceps curls with squats. This will work the biceps here on the front of the arm and also make you stronger for daily activities to be easier like spring gardening and picking things up and putting things down."
The purpose can be
   a. a **<u>biomechanical purpose:</u>** like working the heart for cardio, or biceps for strength
   b. a **<u>functional</u>** purpose, like "improving overall coordination to make movement easier" or "make picking up the groceries easier"
   c. a **<u>mind-body</u>** purpose, like "make you more comfortable in your body-space" or "increase your awareness about your sense of self and universe

2. POSITION: "We're going to stand with our feet the distance of our hip bones with the spine long and strong, weights in the hands, palms up." This really is the stability that precedes mobility, commonly referred to as "exercise setup."

3. PROGRESSION/REGRESSION: "Now we're going to bring the weight closer to the shoulder as we contract. If you want

to make it harder, pronate the palms so the palms face down. This is harder because it involves s a different muscle in addition to the biceps. If you want to make it easier, keep the palms facing up and alternate arms, only doing one arm at a time." This is the mobility we reference when we actually teach the exercise movement. When you make a progression or a regression, items to consider are:

- **lever length**: longer levers are usually harder (eg. Shoulder abduction)
- **bilateral/unilateral** movements: usually doing 2 of something is harder than one of something, esp. with twice weight (eg. Standing bilateral bicep curls)
- **tempo/rhythm**: usually faster is harder (eg. Alternating lunges)
- **bodyweight**: positioning more of the body against gravity usually is harder (eg. Pushup positions)
- **rotation**: usually adding rotation makes a move harder (eg. Abdominal flexions with rotation)
- **stabilization**: usually active, internal stabilization is harder than passive, external stabilization (eg. V sit with and without arms, balancing instead of holding onto something)
- **direction**: usually changing direction increases makes a movement harder

4. BREATH: "Keep breathing, especially try breathing OUT (or exhaling) when the

hands move upward." (The word "prana" comes from the Sanskrit word for "energy," "air," "breath," and "life force." I use the Sanskrit name to keep all of these words starting with the same letter "p" to help me remember them better.

5. T.H.I.E.F.: This is the section where you can interject (time permitting) more talk time with your guest, which is why I call these the class "extras." Cream instructors usually make time to incorporate these three items to make their experience more personal. The acronym "t.h.i.e.f." may assist you in remembering other valuable things you can say to your client.

   The "t" stands for "Transcendence of skills," which means that, now that people are involved in the actual repetitions of mobility (the micro-purpose), you remind them of the bigger picture, the macro-purpose, the functional relationship of how this movement relates to life. For example, continuing our biceps example, you may say something like "all during our day we use our biceps to do things, so if we take care of them, they'll take care of us and our lifting tasks will be easier." Cream coaches teach transcendence of skills. If a client with you demonstrates excellent posture and core control in a hip hinge/dead lift position, but at home brushes teeth over the sink with a rounded back or unsafely bends over to pick something off of the floor, then you have not taught any transcendence of skills. Cream instructors teach both the macro-purpose and micro-purpose of movement.

The "h" stands for "humor" you may wish to incorporate into your experience if your personality so allows. The "i" stands for "interesting," in which you reveal something interesting about yourself by way of conversation, like "I don't have any tattoos on my biceps, but I find them attractive. Mary, what do you think about tattoos around a guy's biceps?" Another example I have recently heard is: "I just saw Nicole Kidman on Access Hollywood and saw her rockin' arms and thought 'that's my motivation for my arms today'."

The "e" stands for "education." Sometimes it is appropriate to take extra time to teach clients something that they otherwise would not have known without you.

The "f" stands for "feeling." More often than not, we get so caught up in the safety and specifics regarding movement that we lose track of where participants should be feeling movement. Cueing where to feel it helps participants zero in on areas of attention. It is more appropriate to ask someone "where do you feel it?" instead of "do you feel it?" because the first must be answered with a specific answer. The second may be answered with a simple nod of the head, but for all we know, when a client says, "I feel it" without specifying a place, the client could actually be feeling it as sharp pain in the lower back and we would never know. For example, you could say: "you should be feeling this in your biceps from the wrists all the way past the elbow."

Cream instructor Patricia Moreno (intensati.com), Founder of IntenSati LIFE in New York City, summarizes all of these "t.h.i.e.f." skills when she teaches. Consistently teaching sold-out classes where she incorporates just as much education as movement, it is not uncommon for her to enter the studio with a non-permanent boldface marker and write the theme of the day's lesson on the studio's mirror with words or phrases. After explaining the purpose, objectives, and theme, she weaves the theme throughout movement, even inviting participants to verbalize some of the words and phrases during the experience (education). At the end of the experience, when she is wiping away the phrases from the mirror, she reviews the theme and objectives from the educational lesson, reiterating the key points she wants her participants to take away from the experience in order to make their lives better (transference). Furthermore, she leaves everyone with a saying that will stay with them, which transcends even the sweat and intensity of movement, such as "remember that life's not measured by the number of breaths you take today, but by the number of moments that take your breath away."

To be sure, the cueing set-up methodology can become time-consuming and complicated. When an instructor spends so much time talking about movement instead of doing movement, he or she wastes valuable workout time for the participants. Carol Scott, instructor and president of the East Coast Alliance (eastcoastalliance.com), says that cueing efficiently is also important. When setting up exercise movement patterns, she gets the class moving first, and then uses verbal and visual cues to refine. "It saves time and allow the participants to get more movement time in." Instructors who get their team moving early can maximize time and also check which modifications and corrections need to be made on that particular day for the group. "Why spend time correcting what students are already doing correctly?," says Scott. Maximize time cueing when problems arrive, not before.

To be sure, this suggested "five step" method to teaching can work for almost any type of class or session. Due to the fast-moving nature of cardiovascular exercise, however, there is little time to do all five steps for each movement of cardiovascular exercise. Sometimes setting out the macro-purpose at the onset is sufficient, such as "remember that even though we're here to burn fat, we're also taxing the heart muscle now to make it stronger later."

MAGIC IN THE MIDDLE

Now that I have scrutinized the major components of the beginnings and closings of the experiences we create, I would like to outline some cream components of excellence in instruction for the middle of our classes and sessions. This, then, is the "meat and potatoes" or "rice and beans" of what cream instructors do that makes them fabulously effective. What takes place in the body of a workout (group or personal) that makes a difference between average milk and cream?

Cream instructors and trainers make their experiences very personal, which involves using the clients' names at least three times in the middle of a session. If this is not possible, then do as much as is feasible. A true sign of confidence in a cream instructor or trainer is when a leader can not only keep abreast of choreography, but also find a way to interject personal anecdotes where appropriate.

When I took a class at a convention from Petra Kolber years ago, it was apparent that something was different from her normal approach. She stopped, looked at the class, and told us about her recent chemotherapy bouts as she was trying to battle Hodgkin's Lymphoma. She invited friend and colleague Lisa Wheeler to the stage to assist her, and she simply cued the rest of the experience while Lisa moved. Instead of trying to pretend that nothing was amiss, she decided to let everyone into the very personal experience of what was going on in her life. Magically, the session peaked with energy to support her, and this session always will be one of the most memorable I have ever attended because of the truth during that workshop.

Cream instructors truly educate their clients, which means that they sometimes do nothing! What? When an amazing dance instructor like Julianne Arney or motivational group fitness leader like Shannon Fable teaches a choreographed pattern of movement, they do not start layering and then continue to layer. Instead, they teach a pattern and then pause themselves while the group continues to practice building muscle memory. They, in fact, do nothing! Surely, they observe movement, cue motivation, and make individual corrections when necessary, but they are true educators because they are instilling independent changes in behavior.

Marcus Irwin also represents the ability to make people responsible for their own movement with what I call the "funnel factor." At the top, a funnel is wide. As liquid pours into a funnel, it narrows and narrows until it comes out of a small hole at the lowest end. At the start of any experience, Marcus uses lots of verbal and visual cueing. As the class continues, he verbally and visually cues less and less, ending up assigning only one word or sound (whistle) for an entire block of 32-count reversible movements. As he funnels his teaching technique from giving more to giving less, he gradually and nonchalantly withdraws as teacher and puts more responsibility on the students as learners. By the end of the experience, he makes but a few sounds and the students have truly learned independent changes in behavior.

Do you remember our definition of education? That can only happen if we "test" them by seeing what behaviors they can do without us.

Have you ever been frustrated as a group leader cueing movement, telling your students to hold a pattern, but noticing that they try to follow you anyway? Oftentimes, I hear "okay, you all keep moving and don't follow me because I'm going to show what comes next." Frustration quickly sets in when we realize that over half of the class tries to follow us. The fault actually is not the students' for not holding their pattern; it is ours.

Let's remember our goal in making education that creates an *independent* change in behavior. The next time you put a client or class in a holding pattern, do nothing! Stop and observe the quality of their movement. When you stop, they quickly become responsible for continuing movement without you, and build muscle memory independently. When you first stop, say nothing. As their movement looks good, you can offer positive, specific feedback, walk around the room, and interact with individuals. Later, when you return to the front of the room and join them in movement, you will have taught them what it means to be in a true holding pattern. You can *now* tell them to continue with what they know—because you have taught it and they can reproduce it independently—while you show a change. The secret to getting a class to be able to hold is to add the little step of *doing nothing while teaching them how to hold*!

We usually incorporate holding patterns as we build up choreography, but building back *down* is just as important. One of the reasons why we break down is to be able to compartmentalize movement and make patterns accessible. Another reason is that we begin with simpler patterns, and invite those who do not want complication to stay in the easier levels of movement. When we change the choreography intensity and complexity, those who want to keep movements simple end up doing an independent routine for much of the class because the majority moves on with the instructor. A cream instructor remembers those in the simpler, more basic progressions of movement and has everyone in the class return to those easier progressions to demonstrate cohesiveness and remind everyone where all the movement started in the first place.

Cream instructors are prepared. This means that they are prepared even for the moments that are less-than-ideal. Nevertheless, cream instructors plan as much of an experience as possible, and this includes transitional movements. For example, if you just finished doing lunges with your class and now want to do something on the floor like push-ups, there are several approaches. One approach is to say "Okay, let's go to the floor and get ready for some chest work," and let the class get to the floor independently. A more polished approach is to say something like: "okay, to get to the floor facing down for our chest work, let's do one more lunge back with the right leg; now let's lower that knee to the floor; now let's kneel; now let's come to all fours; now let's walk the hands forward to a plank position and talk about the setup here for push-ups." The second approach not only *teaches* the class how to move safely, but also moves them in group unison, using fitness moves themselves as transitions.

The following serves as not an exhaustive list, but an aide to get you started thinking about all of the possible options that exist when you transition your students or personal training clients from one position to another. Think about making the transitions themselves part of the workout routine as stand-alone exercises.

From	To	Try this:
seated	Prone	1. 1 hand in front & 1 behind; push to cat; lower 2. take the knees, together, to the same side, and take legs behind the body 3. from SEATED PALM, sit on heels to HERO, and then lower body towards floor with hands, extending legs behind
seated	Standing	1. uncross legs to "hero," then low lunge to high lunge; step together
seated	Supine	1. extend legs to reverse plank; lower 2. "hero"; extend legs; flex elbows
prone	Seated	1. flex hips & knees; come to side; sit 2. push up to cat; cross ankles; sit back
prone	Supine	1. "hero" (come to sitting on heels); push up to reverse plank; flex elbows and lower body 2. roll over 3. see "prone to seated", then "seated to supine" 4. side fetal position; extend muscles; roll to supine
prone	Standing	1. see "prone to seated" then "seated to standing"
standing	Seated	1. warrior 1; "lower lunge," lower knee to floor; sit back 2. kneel to "hero" or cross ankles; sit back
supine	Seated	1. cross ankles; grab knees; rock up
supine	Prone	1. roll over 2. knees to chest; cross ankles, rock up; push forward to cat; lower
supine	Standing	1. see "supine to seated" and "seated to standing"
supine	side-lying	1. raise lower arm and roll onto side
prone	side-lying	1. push up to "plank," turn to one side, lower 2. raise one arm and roll onto that side
kneeling	Standing	1. push forward to "plank," one foot between hands for "lower lunge," stand
kneeling	Supine	1. "reverse plank," lower to elbows & down
kneeling	Prone	1. push forward to "plank," lower 2. "fall and catch" in plank pose 3. Lower to child pose and extend the legs behind you

At the back of the book appears a section detailing some of the most common mishaps of group fitness and some realistic responses.

Rebecca Small from Australia is a cream instructor who is known for her smooth ability to build up choreography from impeccably logical break down skills. Towards the end of most of her hi-lo and step classes, she invites the whole class to do the movements in their simpler form, which mirrors the start of the class without directional changes, intensity hops, and other variations. Not only does this lower intensity gradually, but also: 1. reminds everyone where all the movement came from, and 2. makes everyone again feel part of the same group since some never did the hops, twirls, and leaps.

As I have said, when we study what cream instructors do, the magic more often than WHAT they do is the HOW. The best teachers in the world are not those who come up with the most number of turns, twists, and tangos, but deliver the most simple moves simply. Cream instructors know that less is more. Gin Miller (ginmiller.com), recipient of the 1991 IDEA Instructor of the Year award and creator of Step, is perhaps the most widely known fitness figure globally. She impresses with her moves, but she impresses *more* with her overall style. To be sure, her practical application of science to movement wins awards, but it is her ability to keep movements simple enough for everyone to feel successful that stays with us. Trying to impress with movement (the WHAT) can be forgotten quickly, but impressing with the heart (the HOW) will be remembered.

When we have to teach bilateral movements, cream instructors take advantage of the repetition. A bilateral movement is something that we do to one side that must be repeated to the other side for muscular balance. Step, hi-lo, strength training, and flexibility training like yoga and Pilates are all examples of disciplines where we balance the body between sides.

TRY THIS:

Stand tall with the feet hip-distance apart, hands on the hips. Lunge back with the right leg while simultaneously twisting the body to the left, and return. Repeat with the same leg eight times. Write down here some cues you may wish to include if you were to teach that, using only the categories below that make you feel comfortable. Notice that there is no number 5 because, for 8 lunges, you most probably will not have time for more than this without adding extras. Almost anything you would have cued before you even read this book could fit into any of these categories:

1. Purpose:

2. Position (stability):

3. Progression/Regression (mobility):

4. Prana/Breathing:

Now you have to teach that movement on the other side. Try to complete the following while the class or client does the 8 lunges with the right leg:

5 Things I Could Say That I Didn't Say on the Other Side:
   1.
   2.
   3.
   4.
   5.

5 Things I Could Do That I Didn't Do on the Other Side:
   1.
   2.
   3.
   4.
   5.

Are you stuck? If you are, the following section may assist.

Cream instructors do not repeat themselves, but take advantage of the plethora of tools they possess to keep attention and motivation. I learned years ago that we are like handymen faced with challenges daily to repair in the form of our clients with all of their (and our own) physical issues.

I learned how truly important it is to maintain a varied toolbox of both theory and practical information so that I can always find out how to make the lives of my clients more functional. When I first took Pilates in the last century, I learned so many new techniques for training the abdominals that I wanted to incorporate those into every class I taught. Sadly, I learned that type of flexion and rotation is not for everyone without knowing first more about their abdominal and spinal health. I learned that "if all you have in your toolbox is a hammer, then every class and client will look like a nail." Pilates was my "hammer" and all of my classes for a while were "nails" until I learned about amplifying my toolbox given the wide range of personal differences out there.

Peter Twist (twistconditioning.com), President and CEO of Twist Conditioning Inc., finds that oftentimes trainers use their favorite moves with all clients. "My pet peeve is the OMR training principle – Observe a drill, Memorize it, Regurgitate it to any and all clients – often because the drill is cool or sexy. Trainers should not be focussed on memorizing training "recipes" they replicate

– they should instead take the time and detail to learn how to cook, how to cook a different recipe for each individual.

Our task is to have a toolbox with enough ways to try to fix things that we can always provide personal service based on the needs of our clients and our ability to make modifiable progressions and regressions.

EDUCATION + ENTERTAINMENT = EDUTAINMENT!

DON'T TOUCH THAT STYLE!: exploring the fitness professionals dual roles as educators and entertainers

Part of the challenging role of group fitness instructors and personal trainers is our vast list of responsibilities. All of these combined form the two major categories of our job descriptions: we have to both *educate* and *entertain* clients. *Education* means that clients learn something about themselves during a session or class that they did not know previously. *Entertainment* means that clients come to live sessions and classes because they seek out buzzing energy not unlike that of a live production show. Today's leading instructors and trainers realize this dual nature of the job description and creatively educate and entertain clients and classes in unique ways, and this article poses some unique ways to enhance our ways as entertaining educators.

Elizabeth Larkam (elarkam@wac-clubs.com) is a fitness fusion pioneer, Feldenkrais instructor, and creator of Pilates

Performance. She dedicates herself to the exploration of the intersection of dance and art with dance on Pilates equipment. Elizabeth is an outstanding example of educator-cum-entertainer. When she teaches, precise words flow out of her mouth as if she were giving a lecture on fitness, yet she colors the canvas of her dictionary in such a way that everyone understands what she says. Furthermore, and simultaneously, she entertains through the integration of playful music and interjection of sophisticated humor. It is no coincidence, therefore, that she coined the nouns "edutainment" and "edutainers," fusing the words "education" and "entertainment."

As trainers and teachers strive towards professional improvement, we can gain a deeper insight into the intricacies of the gym floor and classroom by considering these reflective questions:

- "Where is my strength between "education" and "entertainment"?
- "Is my strength in delivering a true experience in *education* so that my participants leave my sessions and classes having learned something that they did not know prior to being with me?"
- "Is my strength in *entertaining* so that my participants never notice the time fly, laugh, interact, and forget themselves

just for a while as if they were spectators in my show?"

From my book *Cream Rises: Excellence in Private and Group Instruction*, the following checklist will help determine your strengths between education and entertainment. While no means exhaustive, the purpose of the two checklists is to get trainers and teachers started on a two-part mission. The first aim is to notice your strengths. The second aim is to seek out specific ways to implement techniques into your sessions from your weaker side, be that educating or entertaining.

Read through the following lists and check off any phrase that specifically *applies to your teaching style on a regular* basis.

EDUCATORS:

☐ I use precise anatomical terms when I teach, and teach my clients and students what these terms mean (examples: "femur," "patella," "ribcage," "ASIS," "coccyx")

☐ I use precise terms of kinesiology (examples: "superior," "abduction," "concentric," "isometric," "sagittal")

☐ I explain the *purpose* of every exercise pattern or movement series

☐ I offer way for everyone to achieve success by incorporating "progressions" and "regressions" as modifications

☐ I explain how to avoid injury during movement patterns

☐ I let the class "in on the secret" of why I choose certain movement patterns and what makes them functional

☐ I explain the transcendence of a particular exercise series for any given day, which means teaching how any particular movement transfers to activities of daily life

☐ I quote recent research or convention information to justify doing something a certain way

☐ I pause to be sure that the client(s) has/have learned an independent change in behavior (example: "if I stop moving, the client or class could continue to demonstrate the required behavior without me")

☐ I may cue specifically like a fitness textbook: "shoulders back and down" as "retract your scapulae with the rhomboids and middle fibers of trapezius; this is called 'scapular retraction'."

◻I make sure that, each time, everyone leaves with at least one new insight or mastery of something and I bring that to their attention at the end of class

◻I ultimately teach people something about themselves

◻I explain major muscles being worked using Latin terms

◻I draw attention to where to feel a certain movement pattern, sometimes using the words "concentrate on," "focus on," and "feel"

◻I may ask thought-provoking, open-ended questions to help participants get in touch with their bodies (examples: "How does this movement make you feel in this area of your body during the concentric phase?")

Please total number of checked boxes here before moving on: ____.

ENTERTAINERS:

☐I may use humor to put everyone at ease

☐I may use personal names of client(s) so that the majority of those in attendance hear their names at least once per class experience

☐I may cue with metaphoric, descriptive language such as "shoulders back and down" as "think of tucking your shoulder blades into the back pockets of your jeans" or "you're in the shower with ice cold water behind you so your shoulder blades react to that"

☐I captivate by their ability to incorporate some or all of the five senses into an experience (examples: I may incorporate taste, aromatherapy, masterfully integrate the music into the experience, and manipulate the lighting at least twice during the class)

☐I may train the client's breath, brain, AND body to some degree in each experience, at least by mentioning each at least once

☐I may choreograph each experience with time, movement, and music, to make magic

☐I put attention into "dressing the part" so that every outfit complements the mood and style of the class and discipline

☐I try to color-coordinate as many aspects of the occasion as possible and feasible (lighting, outfit, equipment, layout, make-up if appropriate)

☐I change the layout of the class from time to time (examples: manipulating the orientation of where the "front" of the room is, changing the orientation of equipment laid out in class like steps or yoga mats, or varying the configuration of students like having them divide into groups, face the back, or form a circle)

☐I change the layout of my direction in regards to the students (sometimes I mirror image, sometimes I face them, and sometimes I stand *next* to them)

☐I break down the traditional barriers between teacher and participants with humor or stories or physical orientation, including using group dynamics so they sometimes can interact with each other

☐I tell a story having nothing to do with the exercise at hand

☐I tell a story including (a) particular participant(s) in the class

☐I change up the way I teach verbally, visually, and kinesthetically so that the "show" is never the same expereince

☐I may change the pitch of my voice, speak louder or softer, and/or sing cues during class

Please total number of checked boxes here before moving on: ____.

MY TOTALS:

____ CHECKED BOXES AS EDUCATOR OUT OF 15

____ CHECKED BOXES AS ENTERTAINER OUT OF 15

As you contemplate the aforementioned questions, you may wish to give the above two lists to a regular client or student of yours and invite his or her impressions of you in order to get someone else's opinion of the same criteria.

Trainers and teachers must hold the attention of all participants, and this involves creating an experience that both teaches and delights. Ankie Feenstra, Pilates instructor and owner of The Bodywork Gym in Mykonos, Greece, agrees, claiming "after we capture that trust and attention, I believe it is our goal to educate them."

Feenstra entertains first, and then educates. "When people come into the Pilates studio," she says, "they always find soft lighting, aromatherapy, and relaxing music. I want them to be comfortable from the very start. During abdominal rotation to the first side, for example, I begin cueing with a friendly, humorous style, saying 'we are going to do some twisting exercises to improve our ability to twist and do a double-take at someone sexy who just walked by on the beach.' This is the instructor as entertainer.

When she has the class rotate to the other side, Feenstra touches her own obliques, incorporating the terms "external obliques," "rectus abdominus," and "spinal rotation" in the process of cueing movements. This is the instructor as educator.

Jay Blahnik, Consultant, Speaker, and Author based in Laguna Beach, California, says he uses the edutainment factor by always looking for ways to provide 'teachable moments' that provide almost invisible education. He outlines, "I incorporate a 'focus of the day theme' in each class, so I can be sure that at least one important educational element will sink in. For example, in my running class, the focus of the day may be 'efficiency.' I invite them to spend time during the workout thinking about ways to be more efficient in posture, foot strike, arm swing and breathing." Setting the stage with a theme provides me permission to educate throughout the workout without seeming overwhelming."

To be sure, the "show" aspect is just as important as the educational aspect. Petra Robinson, Senior Vice president of Zumba based in San Diego, California, says "the Zumba Fitness program emphasizes that instructors are not only educators but performers, entertainers and party hosts to help everyone get lost in the music in creating a simple, fun experience."

Effective instructors as educators remember how they learned difficult terminology, and share their own process of simplification. When veteran aquatics instructor Bernadette O'Brien of New Jersey first learned the concept of "spinal neutral," she found it difficult. "I would cue to them 'keep imagining a long line running down the 7 cervical, 12 thoracic, and 5 lumbar vertebrae' but had a hard time always getting it right. To get my students to be able to remember that, I shared with them how I memorized the number of vertebrae, by associating that I have breakfast at 7, lunch at 12, and dinner at 5." Letting the students "in on the secret" of education signals a cream instructor as educator.

Our roles as "edutainers" come with practice. To be sure, being an "edutainer" means neither being a comedian nor a boring professor. It means motivating and keeping everyone's attention to be on you instead of on the clock. Ultimately, it means doing *whatever* it legally takes to make each experience, to quote Carol Espel, MS, National Director of Group Fitness for Equinox Fitness Clubs, "a *compelling* experience that no participant can afford to miss."

Think about the previous "TRY THIS." Using our 5-part methodology for starters, there are many things you could do while everyone lunges on the right side. They probably do not need to see and hear you stand in the same place and mirror your style exactly. You could leave your spot and walk around to interact with the guests, cue the same thing completely differently (with different language, with only words, with only visual cues, or a combination), incorporate some of the extra t.h.i.e.f. suggestions previously outlined, and many other options.

LANGUAGE

One of the key ways that cream instructors "edutain" is with language. Since we know that more than half of communication occurs based on what is NON-verbal, we also know the importance of choosing words wisely; we have to ensure that what we DO say really counts. Cream instructors speak with impeccable clarity. The opposite of this is what I call the "barf and diarrhea" method of instructing; teachers get it all out, but with no patterned rhyme or reason to their methodology. Scotty Esquibel, Group Fitness Coordinator of the Cooper Aerobics Center for Dr. Kenneth Cooper in Dallas, Texas, teaches with impeccable diction, clarity, and precision. If we were to read a script of any class he teaches, we would understand that there is a conscious choice for every single word. The novices, the blind, the athletes, the arthritic, and the other instructors in the room all could follow his experience based on his words alone. His is the amazing balance of just the right number of words; subtracting one word from his script would leave us in confusion and adding one word would be superfluous. Any blind client would be able to follow his instructions with precision.

When C. Mark Rees (cmarkrees@aol.com), original creator of my company FG2000, Group Fitness Department Head & Life Studio Coordinator in Chicago, cues a client or a class, he maintains a calmness to his voice that is rare. The more excitement that builds in his room with choreography or strength training, the more quiet he becomes, which is refreshing. Instead of yelling, "smile" at his students, he gives them a reason. Instead of screaming at them, he uses a calm voice to invite them to draw on their inner potential and explode with energy. When I am at the most exciting of moments in some of my experiences, before I let temptation get me to scream "go" to everyone, I remember Mark and his uncanny ability to sway a crowd by his calmness. I learned from Mark years ago that maintaining control of a crowd and their energy means that you do not *have* to scream. After all, the only thing worse than screaming at people what to do is *screaming at people what to do into a microphone!*

Mark, like many cream professionals, always counts down. This is more professional than counting up because it prepares students for an upcoming change, lets them know exactly how to gauge their effort, and allows himself not to become a slave to numbers. I could not imagine the

Cape Canaveral rocket launching center in Florida building excitement for a blast-off counting *up*. Of course, exception must be given to dance-based classes that have been relying on a "five-six-seven-eight" cue for dozens of years.

Cream instructors and trainers focus on the positive. Instead of conjuring up a negative example for the brain, they always stay positive, cueing instead to the *solution* not the problem. For example, if I say to you "don't think about a large pink elephant balancing with on leg on a stability ball," the brain cannot help but imagine that which it hears. When we tell our students a negative, the brain first understands that command as a positive, then the brain negates that positive, and this process takes a while. If we just cue what we want, we save time and become more precise in our cueing.

To get out of a habit of saying "don't," I try to remember the word "*keep*." So instead of cuing "don't hold your breath," I cue "*keep* breathing." Instead of cueing "don't round your shoulders forward," I cue "keep the shoulders squeezing towards each other."

TRY THIS:	

Since HOW you say things can mean more than WHAT you actually are communicating, change the following cues from negative cues (problematic) to positive ones (solving) using "keep" or any other words that come to mind to elicit the appropriate change in behavior: For example, instead of "don't forget to breathe," cue "keep breathing."

1. "don't go this way"	

2. "don't let the abdominals pooch out'	
3. "don't let your wrist bend back when you grab the weights"	
4. "don't' let your hips sway back when you stand"	
5. "don't let your hips sag in plank position"	
6. "don't stop"	
7. "don't follow me"	

Making the changes to the table above is only half of the task; making a permanent change in behavior the next time you cue some of those things will be a proven test of education!

INITIATING CHANGE

Some are resistant to change. Predictable, planned formats are hugely successful, as we see with the professional

Les Mills programming structure. Change, however, is necessary in fitness because, the more we train muscles the same way, the less it responds. To those resistant to change, I found two things to say which usually assist me:

1. If nothing changes, nothing changes.
2. To get what we've never had, we have to sometimes do what we've never done.

In my book *The ABC's of Fitness*, I discuss the "vacuum cleaner" syndrome. Whereas a new piece of household equipment may make me sore the first few times I use it, eventually, even as it gets heavier as it holds more dirt, I cease getting sore and actually grow stronger because my muscles are learning to adapt. They become more muscularly efficient (well, at least down one side of my body) because of this change.

The benefits to change are many. Even Les Mills changes its pre-programmed choreography quarterly in an effort to train the body in a new way. A new format will train the brain to react to coordination in a different way. New muscular stimuli train muscles in different ways by changing systems, sets, repetitions, and timing. Different equipment will challenge the way muscular fibers respond to movement patterns. Change can also affect the training of muscular resistance, strength, and hypertrophy. Above all, change ensures that the body can respond to a world that itself is in a state of constant change.

Cream instructors usually hold regular classes, and they also may travel, so having other instructors substitute their classes is common. However, rarely does someone look forward to substituting a class for someone successful because participants can be resistant to change. Cream instructors know that initiating change to some degree on a regular basis teaches students to be prepared for anything. Change, therefore, has an additional advantage of making substitutions far more tolerable. Cream instructors actually prepare their students for change and, consequently, when others substitute for them in their absence, the experience is a positive one.

June Kahn (junekahn.com), AFAA Certification Specialist, Pilates expert, Life Studio Coordinator for Life Time Fitness in Colorado, co-author with me of Human Kinetic's Morning Cardio Workouts, 2009 International IDEA Fitness Instructor of the Year award, and friend, shares her expertise training fitness professionals on a global scale. She also teaches regular classes in Colorado at Life Time Fitness. Because she initiates lots of change in her classes, her students are very comfortable for changing scenarios in education. Even when she is in town, June may invite a qualified colleague to team-teach with her in an effort to expose her students to different teaching approaches. Ultimately, when June is out of town, her students accept substituting instructors with anticipation because they are prepared for change by June's very teaching style. Cream instructors, therefore, teach their students that change is good, that possessing *mental* flexibility to be open to different approaches paves the way for future substitute instructors and trainers. The more instructors who have this mental approach to teaching, the more pleasant the task of substitute teaching will become.

THE FABULOUS FIVE

In our discussion of creating experiences by paying attention to the five senses, I claim that a cream instructor develops skills for both the blind and the participant to enhance both visual and verbal cueing. Now to this list we add three more participants to your experience: your mom (or a mother-like figure), an athlete, and CNN Headline News.

Every time you create an experience for a group, imagine that you have five participants:

1. The blind individual
2. The deaf individual/foreign language speaker
3. Your mom: Imagine that your mother, or a figure like your mother, is in every class. I think about a participant who is eager, positive, enthusiastic about class,

but who may be slightly overweight and have a few body issues like weak wrists, hips, and abdominals. The value of imagining such a figure (whom I always refer to as "Hazel") in every experience is that this keeps us aware of the importance of safety, cleanliness, and, above all, makes us create regressions to make all movement patterns accessible to such participants to create success. Teaching this way avoids someone saying "that was way too hard for me and I can't come back."

4. An athlete: Imagine that an athlete is attending your experience to get some tips on training. I think about a participant who comes ready to move, eager, strong, and looking for a challenging, intense experience. The value of imagining such a figure in every experience is that this keeps us aware of the importance of making progressions in modifications. Teaching this way avoids someone saying, "that was way too easy for me and a waste of my time."

5. CNN Headline News: Imagine that a reporter contacted you the night before the experience and says: "We hear that you are doing amazing things with people and movement in your _____ class. Tomorrow, we

are bringing a film crew to find out what is so special. When we interview you after, we will be asking you three questions: 1. Why you? 2. Why this particular format? 3. Why now (i.e., why is the timing perfect for this experience to be offered now and not last year or next year?). The value to thinking about CNN Headline News attending your class is that you will think about the special factors that make a cream experience. You will pay close attention to the preparation in the details discussed in this book from both the WHAT and HOW of your program.

I developed this methodology of the FABULOUS FIVE years ago when I moved to Puerto Rico to open and manage movement at the Golden Door Spa. Like many facilities, we had only one movement studio, and new spa guests came to our classes every day. I quickly learned that all experiences, regardless what they are called, are really multi-level experiences. Even if a class is called "Yoga Level 2," for example, there always will be at least one individual who should be in a different level. For reasons of instructor, time of day, class length, or friends taking class, people take class for other reasons than just a level specified in a name. In any given timeslot, my instructors soon noticed that attending the same experience would be an athletic "type A" from New York City and a housewife who had never before taken a class but was in the spa redeeming a "Day of Beauty" package.

My cream instructors at the time Carlos Castillo, María Colón, Teodoro Forrestier, Jeff Howard, Rita Maldonado, Grace Muñiz, Lucila Pérez, Emilio Robles, Luís Román, Manuel Velázquez, and Marlene Wiscovitch quickly learned the importance of creating multi-level experiences out of necessity. Indeed, in every experience we had to make regressions, progressions, cue well visually for the international guests who spoke little English or Spanish, cue well verbally, and make every class newsworthy because, indeed, CNN Headline news did visit our spa on several occasions, usually with little or no warning! Managing fitness in that spa environment from 1998 really enhanced my skills as an educator because of the constantly-changing clientele through our golden doors. Imagining these five personalities in every class will help you create experiences that are multi-level, "edutaining," and well-cued. *(For more information on the "fabulous five," check out the article that appears at findLawrence.com clicking on FREE STUFF, then ARTICLES, and see the 2010 Five-Part Series written for IDEA, clicking on the article "5 People Walk into Your Facility.")*

With an understanding of these five people in every group experience or personal training session, you can develop your cueing repertoire to be more varied, thoughtful, and complex, and to this topic we now turn.

CUEING

One of the threads that links the jobs of group exercise instructor and personal trainer is communication: everyone cues. In order to guarantee the richest communication experience for everyone, every time, this review of the three methods for *conveying* meaning can assist fitness professionals to amplify their understanding of three-part cues.

The purposes of cueing are many. Among their uses, cues can reference breathing, rhythm, alignment, numerical order, direction, spatial orientation, movement, anatomical references, spatial orientation, and even humor. The more understanding any communicator has about the three types of cueing, the higher the possibilities for fitness listeners to reach deeper levels of meaning and, consequently, reach goals more efficiently.

All cues can be summarized in the following way. Cueing has been described as "the response you get regardless of intention" (Castells, 2009). Because there are so many individuals who learn (and interpret) in so many different ways, we have to be very varied in our repertoire of how we convey meaning. In group fitness, cueing involves

anything an instructor invokes to convey meaning, which can be in visual, verbal, or kinesthetic form. The overall purpose of cueing in group fitness classes
is multifaceted; the acronym "STEMS" summarizes its uses: S.afety, T.iming, E.ducation, M.otivation, and S.tructureal cues.

• *Safety* involves anatomical, alignment, breathing, and equipment cues.

• *Timing* involves numerical, counting, tempo, and rhythm cues.

• *Education* involves general instruction, relevance, functional purpose, pro- gressing and regressing exercises, and related cues.

• *Motivation* references encouraging, energetic, reinforcement, and even humorous cues.

• *Structure* involves most remaining types of cues that indicate movement, such as execution, direction and spatial cues. It also may include cues about equipment usage during class.

To provide effective cues, GFIs should be aware that each of these types of cues should be delivered via a combination of verbal, visual, and kinesthetic methods to reach as many participants as possible.

The three types of learners are visual, auditory, and kinesthetic. Before attempting a new behavior, the visual learner needs to *see* behavior, the auditory learner needs to *hear* detailed explanations, and the kinesthetic learner needs to acquire a sense of *feeling* something new before mastery occurs. As there are three types of learners, so, too, do three types of cues exits. With visual cues, the communicator demonstrates a desired behavior with body language, making the eyes the main conduit for learning to occur. This student is a "watcher." With auditory cues, the communicator talks a listener through a desired behavior, making the ears the main conduit for learning to occur. This student is a "listener." With kinesthetic cues, the communicator combines visual, verbal, and touching cues so that the receiver acquires an understanding of how a behavior should feel. This student is a "feeler."

While most learners rely on a combination of cueing types for learning to occur, almost everyone has one (subconscious) preferred technique for learning (Faulkner). Unfortunately, there exists no one sure way to determine if one's primary learning preference is visual, verbal, or kinesthetic. One helpful method is to sit in a quiet room with closed eyes, void of sound. Imagine that, to learn a new skill, either recorded descriptions could be played via a sound system, or a video could be played with no sound. One's first reaction to the choice "which would I prefer" helps determine if one's primary learning technique is primarily auditory or visual. An alternative method is to decide one's preference between reading the closed-captions on the evening news on television with the sound muted or listening to the news without looking at the screen.

Effective fitness cuers fuse an understanding of the three different types of learners when they form what Mindy Mylrea calls the "three part cue." Mylrea, recipient of the 2004 Can Fit Pro International Presenter of the Year and of the1999 International IDEA Fitness Instructor of the Year Award, says "the most effective cues contain aspects that address the visual, verbal, and kinesthetic learner so that nobody gets left out." To better understand how to create three part cues, the following sections may help.

The "EYES" the limit! Creating Effective Visual Cues:

All trainers can increase their communication efficiency output if they can imagine their class as deaf or as speakers of a foreign language. Nothing said matters; only visual cues count. Deaf participants rely on everything that they *see* at all times. When cueing for any of the reasons mentioned in the introduction, trainers should try to complement words with appropriate body language to assist in conveying meaning. Yury Miankovich, personal trainer at NShape Vitness based in Hanoi, Vietnam, suggests "just getting into the habit of pointing to the left or right every time we say 'left' or 'right' with the appropriate hand gives visual learners a directional cue. Since I teach to multicultural and multi-language students, visual cueing also helps everyone understand where we're going next from what they *see* instead of me having to choose a specific language." Lyndsay Murray-Kashoid, instructor at Exhale Spa based in Dallas, Texas, agrees. "I also point to muscles on my own body when referencing muscles like 'obliques' and 'latissimus dorsi,' for example, so that everyone at least knows instantly a general area of where we will be targeting. I also use my hands as models to show where and how these muscles contract." Such techniques combine visual aspects of cueing with traditional verbal comments. Figure 1 offers additional examples.

Figure 1
More Visual Cues

When identifying a muscle group like "eretor spinae"	Show with your fingers down your lower neck and spine to the lumbar area to show where these muscles run
When saying "come forward"	Indicate with both hands a forward motion, "calling" the students forward with the hands
When indicating how many more repetitions remain	Indicate this with fingers prominently displayed for all to see
When previewing/demonstrating a move yourself for everyone to see	Invite the class to face you first to enjoy greater visual access, possibly indicating those in front to be on the floor and those towards the back of

	the room to stand
When giving positive feedback	Indicate this visually with a "thumbs up" sign, smile, or other visual feedback

Run to your "EARS!" Creating Effective Auditory Cues:

Trainers can heighten an awareness of visual cues by choosing sentences as if their class were blind. Blind students require succinct and precise cues. Commonly hard fitness cues like "good job," "do it this way," and "if that's too difficult, try this," are non-specific cues that alienate rather than invite because a blind person (and verbal learner) would not be able to follow. "I try to make my cues short and specific enough," Miankovich agrees, "so everyone can follow me on my voice alone, especially at times when they can't see me, like in downward-facing dog."

When choosing words, Neuro Linguistic Programming tells us that tone and body language are just as important as the words themselves (Morgan). With tone alone there are over a dozen ways to say the four words "We're gonna do squats." Word choice also counts: words themselves should be positive. In an effort to cue to the solution without referencing potential problems, avoiding the word "don't" keeps a focus on the desired behaviors. Jeremy Koerber, author of *101 Ways to Improve Your Personal Training Business,* agrees, stating "just cueing what you want avoids spending time focusing on negative behaviors you want to avoid anyway. Instead of 'don't hold your breath,' I suggest 'keep breathing,' or, instead of 'don't let your knees go past your toes in the squats,' I use 'keep the knees behind the toes when you sit back.'" Cueing in the positive realm helps everyone focus on desired results faster. Figure 2 offers some additional examples of effective verbal cues.

Figure 2
More Verbal Cues

Instead of cueing "don't"	Use the word "keep" to focus on the solution (i.e., "keep breathing" over "don't hold your breath")
Instead of over-cueing possible mistakes	Only make verbal corrections to the errors you see present
Instead of cueing "straight" spine or "flat" back (which would be anatomically unnatural positions)	Cue more effective, educational, and professional words like "neutral," "long and strong," "elongated," "pulled," and "lengthened"
Instead of using habitual cues like "navel to spine"	Create more innovative cues that make participants react to something new like "you have to fit into some really tight pants for a photograph, so use your core muscles to shrink your waistline and support your spine"
Instead of cueing "modification"	Try using words like "level 1" or "regression" to decrease complexity or intensity and

which can be negative and non-specific	"level 3" or "progression" to designate an increase

Leaving Impressions in the "HANDS" of Time: Creating Effective Kinesthetic Cues:

The third type of cueing, kinesthetic cueing, addresses all five senses with an emphasis on touch.   Where the visual learner needs to *see* what an exercise is, and the verbal learner needs to *hear* where an exercise take place, the kinesthetic learner needs to *feel* an exercise. Some learners profit the best from a combination of both verbal and visual cues, requiring a more complete cueing experience. These kinesthetic learners do best when they relate to both where and how they are supposed to feel a certain exercise in their own bodies. Cuers should both incorporate the word "feeling" with visual cues, indicating on their own body parts where sensations should occur when teaching movement. "During abdominal crunches," begins Miankovich, "I not only show on my own body where the muscle runs to help them identify the focus of the exercise, but also tell them that they should feel a strong attraction activation down the front of the torso, between the ribs and the hips."

The kinesthetic learner needs to understand how everything comes together for a particular feeling. The kinesthetic approach to cueing involves telling participants both *where* they should feel movements and *how* these movements should feel. Depending on the regulations of each specific club and country, a gentle touch to a client on a key body part (with the client's permission) may enhance further the participant's kinesthetic learning (Rothenberg).

Advantages to understanding the kinesthetic learning process include corrective techniques. Corrections for kinesthetic learners sometimes require instructors to interact on a more personal level. The technique of putting one's hand to the solution and inviting a participant to move towards the hand works wonders. Consider, for example, a client in a plank position whose hips are too high, neck out of alignment, and knees asymmetrical. When the trainer approaches the client at knee level and puts his or her hand below the ASIS part of the client's hips at the desired level, saying "Jeffrey, can you lower your hips just to my hand please?" this allows the client to take responsibility of his own kinesthetic awareness to move towards the solution without the trainer having to touch the client. Repeating the same procedure with the trainer's palm and the client's chin and knees offers the kinesthetic client a tactile point of reference for both present and future correction. Trainers who get into the habit of putting their hands at the places they want their clients to move *towards* help train kinesthetically.

Trainers and instructors should aim to form three-part cues by imbuing a visual, auditory, and kinesthetic aspect into each major cueing experience. Three-part cues help communicators reach the widest amount of learners possible because these cues incorporate the three types of learning. Personal trainers and group fitness instructors alike who get into the habit of using the three-part cue with their clients and classes help guarantee the success of everyone by encompassing a wide variety of learning possibilities.

Self-Discovery

To improve one's mastery of the three-part cue, trainers and instructors should acquire permission from a client or class to videotape all or part of a session for the leader's private use. Watching the recorded session three times will assist any educator in refining these cueing techniques. The first time, the observer should watch the recording with the sound muted. Ask "Would I be able to follow this based only on what I see?" The second time, the observer should listen to the recording without looking at the video. Ask "Would I be able to follow this based only on what I hear?" The third time, the observer should play the video with attention to both sound and vision. Ask "How does the overall combination of visual and verbal cues create a meaningful experience?" "In which areas of cueing could I improve?"

Constantly updating one's own personal repertoire of verbal, visual, and kinesthetic cueing will keep experiences fresh with both clients and classes. These suggestions for effective communication skills will help decrease the possible confusing gaps between the cuer's mind and the participants' movements.

The best cues are three-part cues.

CAREER DEVELOPMENT

On a daily basis, I get emails from individuals asking me for career development suggestions. The question is always one of three:

1. Where and how did you get started in fitness?
2. What are the steps you recommend to me to further my career in my own area?
3. I want to be a presenter. What are the steps I should take?

I always begin by emailing each fitness professional a prepared file I have that answers each of these questions. Those responses will follow here. For the professional requesting more in-depth mentoring, I also began providing mentoring services through my company, Fitness Group 2000, for individuals wishing to have me work through their career development on a personal basis with them, using my contacts and abilities to help them move along the industry faster. There is always information available about personal mentoring available on my site at findLawrence.com.

Let's look at the answers to the three most common questions that come my way:

1. Where and how did you get started in fitness?

My fitness mission has been to show others how I changed my life from being an overfat youth to surviving anorexia as an adolescent male. During eight years of Catholic education, I would come home from school and have dinner. Between that and bedtime was usually a half gallon of ice cream (chocolate chip mint) with television shows, and homework. It was easy to put on weight with this sort of lifestyle. In high school, I went in the other direction and almost stopped eating during those years as I battled anorexia at a time when it was completely undiagnosed in the male population.

As I began my first week of college, my father died of heart disease when I was 18 in 1983. That shocked me into thinking about taking care of myself since not only was I grossly underweight and underfed, but I realized that I had also inherited some of his heart problems. A few years later, my mother had open-heart surgery, and shortly after that, my only brother died instantly of a heart attack at 38. I learned early that I had inherited many physical problems, but have tried to share with others the techniques I used in changing my own life in an effort to inspire.

As I became meta-conscious about the process of getting healthy again with food and movement, others began asking me in college to share my "success secrets" with them. I never competed in fitness as so many of my colleagues; indeed, I was clumsy, inflexible, weak, and uncoordinated as I began to get fit. Most of the "stars" I know in fitness today at this time were competing all over the world and I was just starting to teach "aerobics" in college to others who wanted to start fitness on campus. My first loves of classes to take were aquatic fitness (because I could hide mostly in the water and not realize how much I was sweating) and T'ai Chi on land (because it was not aggressive like football, moved really slowly, and was non-competitive).

Throughout graduate school working towards my two Masters of the Arts degrees, I continued to teach to students and faculty. After doing fitness as a hobby for many years, I became a full time fitness professional in Dallas, Texas, driving all over the city to teach classes. Soon, I started giving workshops to local facilities, and gradually began looking beyond my zip code.

For continuing education, I knew that the IDEA convention would be my one-stop shop of fitness resources, so I saved money to go to the annual WORLD convention. While I felt so out of place and uncoordinated in *classes taught by Keli Roberts and Jeff Vandiver, I thrived on this energy and somehow felt at home.*

Back home, I honed my personal mission to assist others because I would simply share how I helped myself. To be professional, I attended the first ACE Certification Exam in Washington, D.C., and became gold certified as the first-time-ever group of professionals sat down for that exam. At the insistence of my classmates, I began applying to conventions to present classes beyond my local area. Nobody replied positively, and I have kept every single rejection letter I ever received because it reminds me of the important role of determination. Whenever I felt daunted about my lack of qualifications and experience at home, I remember that Dr. Seuss had to apply his books with twenty-two rejections before the twenty-third publisher said yes, and he never had a single kid of his own at home.

If any of this story interests you, my first book, *The One-Percent Factor, an Eccentric Unicorn's Guide to Touring and Traveling,* available at findLawrence.com, has a chapter dedicated to each of the preceding paragraphs.

2. What are the steps you recommend to me to further my career in my own area?

To address career growth, you have to be both popular and professional. The business side of fitness means that, plain and simple, classes should be successful, which at most facilities and timeslots is defined as "full." To be popular, the single best resource I can point to in order to be popular is amass all of the tips and techniques included in this book.

To be professional, group fitness leaders need to possess a current, valid, internationally recognized group fitness certification. To be professional, personal trainers need to possess a current, valid, internationally recognized personal training certification. If one wishes to do both, then one needs to have a certification in both disciplines. Getting a certification is half of the responsibility: maintaining it <u>current</u> is the other. Group fitness managers and personal training managers who hire should validate with certifying bodies that individuals claiming to be certified indeed <u>are</u> currently certified. This validation process keeps the system of hiring in our profession ethical.

As the fitness arena changes regularly, I recommend attending at least one major personal training or group fitness convention per every two years, either accomplished at one time, via several smaller workshops, or with a combination of home-studies. If financial reasons prevent this, I recommend asking employers to subsidize your continuing education. You may also apply for a BISCONTINI SCHOLARSHIP at findLawrence.com for convention expenses.

Step 1: BE CERTIFIED. I recommend AFAA (afaa.com) and ACE (acefitness.org) as starting certifications. If, however, travel to a certifying city is problematic, you may wish to consider first a home study specialty certificate from scwfitness.com and afpafitness.com. Other group fitness and personal training certifications exist: please consult findLawrence.com/LINKS.php for other respected examinations.

Step 2: BE PREPARED. Decide what your message, mission, and contributions to the arena of fitness education will be. Create a workshop that fuses both theory and practice. Use a leading professional's workshop template as a way to get started writing your outline. I suggest basically dividing your workshop outline into two halves: the first half represents the theory and the second represents the practical application of that theory.

Step 3: WORK IT. Present this workshop for free in a local facility for the experience and feedback you will get on the evaluations. Invite your colleagues. You may also wish to tie the workshop in some way to charity, in which in lieu of payment people bring old coats, shoes, or canned goods, for example. Promote yourself in a facility as a professional offering a free workshop, and tell participants what they will receive: choreography, ideas, exercises, research, energy, motivation, etc. At this point, you most probably won't be offering any continuing education credits.

Step 4: RE-WORK IT! To get feedback, feel free to use an evaluation similar to that on the following page. Read your feedback immediately after you present your workshops and decide then and there which parts of your workshop, outline, or both, you would like to amend. Always begin an email database of those who attend your workshops so that 1. You can email them personally immediately after to express your gratitude, and 2. You can use this database to promote future workshops.

CLASS OR SESSION EVALUATION
Thank you for attending today. Please be HONEST as I will use this feedback in order to make this workshop the best it can be!

Date:

Course Name:

Instructor(s):

Evaluate these categories from 1 to 5 (where 5 is the best score possible):

1. Instructor's knowledge/mastery of subject:
   O1 O2 O3 O4 O5
2. Instructor's organizational skills
   O1 O2 O3 O4 O5
3. Instructor's overall communication & presentation skills:
   O1 O2 O3 O4 O5
4. Instructor's Customer Service:
   O1 O2 O3 O4 O5
5. Today's material was appropriate for today's students:
   O1 O2 O3 O4 O5

Other comments, observations:
WHAT I LIKED MOST WAS: _____
_____
_____
WHAT I LIKED LEAST WAS:_____
_____
_____

Step 5: APPLY IT! Become a provider for ACE and AFAA. Go to their respective websites (listed above) and download their Provider Applications. You are much more marketable in the industry if you can offer BOTH ACE and AFAA credits. In addition, any other certifying bodies accept the credits of ACE and AFAA as well, like ACSM accepts ACE credits. To be a provider for each, with little exception (like a degree in your fitness field), you must be certified by each. Prepare your outlines and submit your applications with all necessary paperwork and payments. When you have been approved as a faculty provider, continue with step 6.

Step 6: PROMOTE IT! Promote your revised workshop beyond your local facility, attracting fitness professionals within at least a ten-mile radius of your zip code. Choose a very low price to make the workshop attractive. Remember, you are still using this time as practice time as you hone your skills at presenting and look for constructive feedback. Be sure to promote ACE and AFAA credits on your advertising material. I recommend starting with a three to four hour workshop offering two to four continuing education credits, based on how much movement (if any) versus theory your workshop contains. (Relax: ACE and AFAA decide this for you based on your outlines when you apply).

Step 7: EVALUTE IT! This time, you've made money. Consider your evaluations carefully to be sure you have given value for money, fulfilled all promises made by your promotional materials, and done your best work yet. Again, return to your outline and workshop content after reading your evaluations and make any necessary changes.

  Step 7: Consider offering your workshop to your entire state or country. Mailing lists are available from ACE and AFAA.

  Step 8: Become more marketable by creating a second workshop! Repeat steps 1 – 8. ☺

  3. I want to be a presenter. What are the steps I should take?

  First, be SURE of your message. When you are going to present, remember that your application will come in on any given day to any given company with no less than ten other applications for your discipline, be it cardiovascular, strength, or flexibility, a combination of those, a mind-body focus of those, or a traditional focus of those. CONSTANTLY ASK YOURSELF HOW YOU STAND OUT IN THE INDUSTRY AS YOU APPLY.

  Next, do all of the steps under question #2 above until you have at least three amazing workshops that are all approved for ACE and AFAA credits.

  Attend conventions and introduce yourself with business cards to EVERYONE (presenters and colleagues) in a networking effort.

Consider a website or at least electronic press kit. Check out mine at findLawrence.com. Consider a professional fitness mentor. Always ponder; Think about your workshops and think about your mission. Hone with colleagues or your mentor the fine balance between being REALLY GOOD at a few things yet simultaneously developing a DIVERSE packet of workshops.

Contact fitness convention websites and fill out the Presenter Applications, either from downloaded packets or online with internet connection. A huge advantage of working with a fitness mentor occurs now. When you apply, your fitness mentor also emails the prospective fitness convention to recommend and endorse you as a presenter because you have been mentoring with an already known talent. This proves to be a huge advantage in the industry to separate you from hundreds of other applicants from your same discipline.

MISTAKES

Many words describing fitness begin
with the letter "p":

- Patient
- Peaceful
- Peace-making
- Permissive
- Personable
- Philosophical
- Playful
- Plentiful
- Poetic
- Policy keepers
- Policy breakers
- Posers
- Poignant
- Practice
- Presence
- Preventive
- Primadonna (well...)
- Proficient
- Progress
- Progression
- Progressive
- Polish
- Prophetic

However, one word that cannot
describe even the cream instructor is
"perfect." The best of the best is not immune
to imperfections, whether they come from
external sources such as other individuals
and technical difficulties or internal sources
like our own mistakes and weaknesses.

When we teach, we grow. Mistakes are part of life; so learning from mistakes can be a wonderful experience. When I evaluate instructors, I try to point out ways for them to grow. I tell them that I always expect to see mistakes, but never the SAME ones. The point is to grow.

Some of my most powerful mistakes in the arena of group and personal training have also been my most powerful lessons. Following is but 7 lessons I have learned from each area.

GROUP FITNESS:

1. Insanity is defined as "doing the same thing over and over expecting something to change." I went through a phase in group fitness where I used to think that my students would leave my classes if I did the same thing over and over, so I constantly changed everything so much so that nobody ever felt comfortable in class; every day was an entirely new experience. Then I learned from programs like Les Mills that participants like to be comfortable with routines so they can better gauge their strength and energy. The lesson I learned over time was that my style would be a happy medium between the two extremes of having a predictable format and style on one hand and including enough changing elements

135

in an experience to keep people entertained.

2. After teaching classes, I used to ask people "did you get a great workout?" Not always did people answer me with a "yes." Sometimes, they would say, "class wasn't hard enough" or "last Tuesday was more intense." My ego would be wrecked until the day I realized that, as a certified professional, I keep myself trained, develop the exercise prescriptions, and continually re-evaluate ways to be an effective edutainer. I learned that I cannot hold myself responsible for their intensity as well. Looking at them after class, I used to decide that they worked hard enough if they had worked up a sweat. I later learned that sweat usually measures more humidity than intensity, and people can work up a huge sweat just standing in a steam room and doing nothing at all. I learned that guests are responsible for their own intensity. More importantly, I learned that, instead of waiting for class to finish to ask them if they 'got a great workout,' I tell them at the start of each experience: *"at the end of this experience, the ultimate question will be 'did you give yourself the intensity that you needed today, for you'."*

3. There was a phase I went through in choreography where I believed that the best teachers presented the most complicated moves in an effort to "test" only the best students in the class. Later,

I learned that true edutainers take their educational role seriously. Their role is to teach to those even in the back row: to create an inclusive, not exclusive, experience for all. The lesson I learned was that, apart from safety, the most important word in any experience for group or personal training is *success*.

TRY THIS:

Review in your mind the last personal training or group session you taught. Try to picture the entire segment as if you watched the scene play on a dvd. Ask yourself how successfully each participant *moved*. Ask yourself how successfully each participant *felt* at the end of the experience. Remember this word *success* each time you work with people and challenge yourself to raise the bar in order to make success a more important theme each time.

4. I used to try to create classes with lots of challenging movement. I loved it when participants grunted from effort. I thought that making complicated routines and difficult movements were signs of great instructors. I never really heard these instructors reference the WHY of what they were doing, however. After starting to work for AFAA, I learned to question the *purpose* of movement. The lesson I learned from starting that relationship was to question the *purpose* of everything in fitness, from group to personal training. I also made it my

mission to explain the purpose to as many aspects of an experience as possible.

5. I used to spend lots of time preparing for my classes. I would write out choreography, plan my outfits, and coordinate my music. When I was with my personal training clients and classes, I would assume the role of the script I prepared just for that class. Whether participants had *success* or not, whether people followed or not, I did not pay much attention: I wanted to be true to what was planned in my head. When some participants left because they felt that I taught classes that were too hard or intense, I was faced with a choice: be strict to my 'script' or learn to make changes on the spot as needed to allow more participants to feel successful. I learned the value of being able to "ATM" or "abandon the mission." This means doing whatever it takes on the spot to present a successful experience for the majority of the participants in the room. To be sure, there will almost always be one or two participants who never will quite "get it," but we should teach towards the success of the majority. I have been privileged enough to appear at conferences where leading choreographer to the stars Tony Stone appears. After sessions backstage, he tells a story of often hearing presenters come offstage and complain about the "level" of participants in any given country. When such presenters complain, Tony defends the instructor's true role, saying that "the outstanding presenter's role is to evaluate

the level of the participants in **_any_** venue and immediately adapt skills in order to make the experience one of **_success_**. Complain about the level?" he says, "WE have to match **_their_** level." When presenters have submitted choreography notes months in advance, they oftentimes fall into the trap of believing that they have to follow their aspirations conceived at a computer months before. More important is assessing the level of the group and then teaching to that very level. When standing live before participants cream instructors should pull movement patterns that not only stimulate and challenge, but also make **_success_** a key outcome, regardless of what is printed in the program manual. If a presenter envisioned creating an experience that will not work in the current environment, he or she needs to adapt instantly to the abilities of the majority.

6. I used to be the combination of parrot and dog. Like a parrot, I would clone the routines and movements of others, and like a dog I would bark those orders to others. After attending conventions around the world, I learned the value of edutaining, of combining education with entertainment in a flowing manner. Today I find it very common to attend classes, workshops, and personal training sessions that separate theory and practice. There is usually either lots of talking for a while and then lots of movement for a while. The lesson I learned from an educational perspective is that

people will learn more when they are given small amounts of theory combined immediately with small amounts of practical application. I started incorporating that format into my workshops for fitness professionals: perhaps ten to fifteen minutes of theory followed by ten to fifteen minutes of practical demonstration that immediately demonstrates that theory. Most importantly, I learned to remind them where to feel movements. It seems to me that, so often, we become guilty of telling our classes and clients so much *what* to do that we neglect to tell them *where* to feel it. Furthermore, we should never ask our clients the closed-end question "do you feel it?" They could nod, we move on, and nobody would be more certain of anything. If, however, we ask them "where do you feel it," this gives them the opportunity to tell you exactly where they feel it, which is important. During abdominal curls, for example, we would want a client to tell us that she feels the movement in the front of her core, but not feel pain in her neck or lower back.

7. When I began taking classes, I rarely felt successful. I always felt that teachers were giving movements to everyone *except* for me. I did not ever find that teachers were accessible, real people. The lesson I learned from this was to teach movements for real people, involving them in the *process* over the product, also letting them in on the *why* we move. This means remembering when I was new to fitness the movements like

pushups that were challenging for me, and how I got through it. Cream instructors never lose sight of the process of being there themselves.

PERSONAL TRAINING

1. When I began personal training, I wanted to be successful, which to my ego meant that my clients were achieving their goals. When they were not all meeting their goals, I felt dejected. Following the tips of great personal trainers like Sheri and Alex McMillan, I learned that, many times, the fault was not in my training program, but in my initial mindset. The lesson here was that I could only help my clients achieve their goals if we made sure from the start that their goals were *realistic*. In Puerto Rico at the Golden Door Spa, it is not uncommon for clients to book me for a first-time personal training session with a list of goals in one hand and a cigarette in the other, asking to learn to lose ten pounds, reshape their body, quit smoking, and learn how to eat, all in one introductory session. I jokingly tell them that my job is a "mind-body personal trainer" and not a dreamweaver for the Make a Wish Foundation. On a serious note, I learned that one of the initial tasks of today's personal trainer is to set realistic goals and redefine them often.

    Along with making realistic goals, I learned that simply holding a certification was no substitute for experience and deeper education in getting people healthier. Peter Twist summarizes the importance of integrity in education in learning and sharing information. He says that, in the US and in Canada, "legally trainers aren't required specific schooling or specific certifications to be permitted to label themselves as 'personal trainer' and begin their practice. Sometimes we have a resulting zero academic integrity. Because trainers do not have to have university degrees, the awareness of the academic process (from research to peer reviewed publications to professional magazines to books to the readers and practitioners) basic academic integrity of referencing material etc is had been demolished. Oftentimes, trainers learn in courses then copy and paste copyrighted material verbatim on their web sites, in brochures, and even in articles and presentations too. There is a little too liberal gleaning of information – shared with the goodwill of educators; stolen and misrepresented by trainers as their own words."

2. I used to train muscles in isolation because clients wanted to see endurance and hypertrophic changes in their bodies. With the onset of functional training, however, I learned that it is far more useful for everyday life to train for movements over muscles, and function over physique. I am much more rewarded when a client tells me that she can now bend over to pick up the large bag of flour from the lowest shelf in the grocery

store herself than I am when a different client tells me his biceps are getting bigger.

3. I used to cue my clients telling them what NOT to do. Instead, I learned to cue in the positive realm, omitting the word "don't" from my vocabulary. There is more on this type of positive cueing in the verbal cueing section of this book. More than just a lesson in using words, this tip keeps a positive focus for encouraging and empowering mental imagery as well.

4. When I began tracking the progress of my personal training clients, I had my paper and pen in hand, standing at the ready to write down numbers of dates, sets, reps, and weights. I learned that people are more important than numbers, however, and began to start to write down words as well to track their progress. To be sure, the traditional ways we write down their progress is important, but I also added adjectives they give me describing such categories as "mental outlook today," "energy," "what thoughts are consuming you today," etc. I started tracking feelings in addition to numbers. These words provide an additional helpful tool to use when tracking a client's progress over time and re-evaluating goals.

5. So often we progress our clients to be able to increase endurance, hypertrophy, number of repetitions, or overall weight, for example, but we neglect to praise the progress. My lesson, therefore, was to learn to point out progress with each client to some degree

every day, however small. I try to find one thing to complement that shows an overall improvement and verbalize that. What we may take for granted may be a huge step for the client, and praise could foster an even increased motivation. Traditionally, personal trainers work their clients' muscles to the point of exhaustion. Feeling this exhaustion can oftentimes be enough to make a guest feel "not strong enough" to continue, with some potential physical *and* emotional effects. Extra reassurance that temporary weakness can be a sign of permanent strength gains is a positive part of growing ensures success on all accounts.

6. Many times, many of my highly-motivated personal training clients ask me for ways to lose weight or for exercises to do on their own without me to help them reach their goals faster. I used to have pre-made handouts featuring lists and lists of ways to burn more calories for my clients. Unfortunately, some clients overtrained and showed symptoms of fatigue. While I encourage self-motivated movement, I know that overtraining can lead to injury and a host of other physical complications, so a valuable lesson I learned was to encourage *resting as hard as training.* In our Human Kinetics book *Morning Cardio Workouts,* June Kahn and I have developed an entire chapter dedicated to easier, less-intense mind-body cardiovascular workouts suitable for recovery days, such as mind-body walking.

7. When I work out in the gym with my own routine, I love to focus on the interactions other personal trainers have with their clients. They fascinate me when they get their clients to do creative, multi-joint, triplanar movement patterns safely and effectively. I always ask myself, however, first, if the client actually understands the "purpose of the pattern," and, second, if the trainer encourages independence with the client. This means: could the client do the same movement pattern just as well without the trainer? Some trainers fear their clients' independence. I started out trying to make my clients dependent on my programs, saying things like "Next Tuesday we will really change your body with a new approach to chest training" or "Don't' try the stuff we did today until we're back together because I want to supervise your movement to be sure you're doing everything well." I feared my clients' independence. By seeing successful trainers with unbelievably long waiting lists like Nicki Anderson, Juan Carlos Santana, and Paul Chek, I learned not to fear client independence.

Actually, the more independent you make clients, the more they talk to others about the increased quality of their lives, and, consequently, the more your waiting list fills up as a personal trainer with others wanting you to do the same thing for them. If you truly are a functional trainer, then you are teaching every client the *relevance* of each movement to activities of daily life and, in turn, ensuring independence. Rita Maldonado (<u>rmaldonado@luxuryresorts.com</u>), Fitness Supervisor of the Golden Door Spa in Puerto Rico, says that the "best leaders render themselves unnecessary." This means that true educators have instilled a permanent, independent change in behavior in clients. Clients become empowered and independent, which I believe should be the ultimate goal of every mind-body personal trainer.

The preceding 14 lessons I share with you as a bit of autobiographical history in my relationship with fitness. I have learned great lessons from these mistakes, and I share them now in order to empower more excellence in education so more people can avoid the same mishaps.

Making the most out of your abilities to teach and train, then, takes practice. United, the tips posed among the pages of this book could take years to master. I suggest you begin with any single tip found on these pages and implement that. After you feel comfortable making one change, add a different teaching tool. To be sure, it can seem at first very daunting when you read a book like this with so many tips for embellishing the way you educate.

List here five techniques you read in this book that you would like to implement in your career, whether now or in the future:

_____

_____

_____

_____

_____

_____

The remaining sections of the book deal with special topics: mind-body personal training, mindfulness, web wisdom, management of cream instructors and personal trainers, uncommon solutions to common issues, mishaps, specific take-away suggestions, and some answers to some of the workbook-style questions asked in earlier sections.

FOR PERSONAL TRAINERS: MINDFUL PERSONAL TRAINING

The diagram I proposed at the outset of this book outlines the person as a trilogy of brain, body, and breath (traditionally referred to as "mind, body, spirit.") In order to stay on top of this trend today, today's personal trainer addresses all aspects of this trilogy in training. If we accept the premise that a personal trainer trains a person, and a person is a trilogy, today's personal trainer should train the trilogy.

The job description of the personal trainer has evolved more around the recent turn of the century than perhaps in over thirty years previously. To be sure, personal trainers everywhere are still concerned with a kinesiological approach to the human constitution, but the fitness arena in which they work has evolved so dramatically in recent years that their role has been required to transcend that of a mere "equipment manager." The plethora of "softer" forms of fitness such as yoga, Pilates, T'ai Chi & Chi Gong, Feldenkrais, Alexander Techniques, Lotte Berk, Resist-A-Ball©, meditation classes, and Aqua Mind-Body classes permanently have invaded our arena and, consequently have broadened the expectations of our clients more than ever. Clients, therefore, are not only more educated, but they also have come to depend on an effective personal trainer who not only trains their bodies, but who also helps guide their minds as well. The personal trainer's role, then, has evolved to one of personal coach that should draw, not only from the more traditional cardio-muscular approaches, but also to some degree from these aforementioned disciplines that focus on the ever-present concept of *mindfulness*. To survive and thrive in today's business market, the personal trainer must maximize his or her approaches to mindful training, meaning the incorporation of mind-body approaches to fitness into what used to be traditional program prescriptions in an effort to address each client in the new millennium more holistically.

Closer inspection of the adjective "personal" in "personal trainer" reveals the noun "person" inside. This "person" is comprised of mind, body, and spirit. Close inspection of the roots of the word "spirit" date to Latin and Greek "spiritos," meaning "breath." The "spirit" aspect of fitness for the purposes of this book, therefore, refers to the incorporation of a mindful awareness of the breath. The effective personal trainer, therefore, must address in every session the brain, body, and brain, to some degree. To be sure, the words "mind-body-spirit" fitness conjure up discomfort in some. It may help to reword that trilogy with "brain-body-breath" fitness in an effort to reach more in comfort.

Drawing from current research, an overview of current, popular mind-body techniques, and the helpful acronym "n-a-ma-s-t-e," this lesson strives to give the personal trainer realistic, tangible techniques from mind-body applications to assimilate into existing personal training programs almost immediately. Since the personal trainer trains the person, and this "person" consists of mind, body, and spirit, today's personal trainer by syllogism, therefore, must address, to some degree, the training of each client's mind, body, and spirit in each session.

CURRENT RESEARCH AND TRENDS

Most respected voices in the industry such as Chek, Cibario, Seabourne, and Kravitz, agree that repeated traditional isotonic exercise of a muscle group causes increased *inhibition* over time of the stabilizers that cross those joints. Personal trainers collectively are discovering the great benefits from slower training, a decreased use of flat-bench training, and less repetitions. Furthermore, that muscular adaptation to stimuli is extremely efficient and serves as constant motivation for the effective personal trainer to strive for variety in client training. One of the most significant results from a program with increased variety is the amount of time that remains freed up from a typical session. Since the goal nowadays is muscular *integration*, and not isolation, functional training allows both prime movers and stabilizers to fire simultaneously during a workout, thereby minimizing time traditionally used in lengthy, separated, isolation exercises, taking individuals from machine to machine. Clients are spending less time on separate exercises and more time integrating their bodies as functional units.

The plethora of new equipment on the market helps personal trainers integrate functional training and mindfulness. Stability/mobility balls, medicine balls, wobble boards, Reebok Core Boards, and Bosu equipment all have invaded our fitness centers, and they're here to stay. These pieces of equipment help trainers depend less on the traditional pieces of costly machinery and train the body in a more integral approach. As we set behind the traditional machine-dependent sitting training, the trainer now has more time without having to do a mandatory machine circuit. Truly, the trainer is freer now to embrace a more active type of training from the more traditional isolation training.

In this free time, the personal trainer can now incorporate some mind-body approaches to fitness throughout the overall approach to each client. In addition to addressing a client's specific muscular concerns, the effective personal trainer of the millennium must also dedicate himself or herself to the very goals addressed in mind-body fitness. These are: improving flexibility, balance, reaction time, the ability to do work safely and efficiently in *various* types of challenging environments, and the ability to achieve and maintain wellness and peace. Truly, the personal trainer's job description has evolved, but these are fast becoming the expectations of future clients.

First Things First: Learning New Trends by Experiencing Some Really Old Ones

Nothing can be taught that is not experienced. Personal trainers wishing to incorporate some mind-body approaches to fitness must first expose themselves to a plethora of stimuli from as many different mind-body venues as possible. A personal trainer should take at least two classes in the following from different teachers each time: yoga, Pilates, T'ai Chi, Feldenkrais, Alexander Techniques, Lotte Berk, Resist-A-Ball©, meditation, Guided Meditation, and Aqua Mind-Body classes. The point is not to take a "crash course" in foreign teaching methods to become a different trainer, but both to experience classes that address more than the physical body of a client, and to learn from the cognitive *teaching* approaches exemplified in mind-body classes.

Personal trainers should pay attention to how calmly and personally yoga teachers traditionally greet and escort their guests as they walk into a room, and to their relaxing tone of voice during a class. Trainers can harvest ways to assist clients with necessary breathing techniques that prove so important during weight-bearing exercises. Effective yoga teachers also should be observed for instilling genuine self-awareness and postural alignment corrections to participants. Assisting a client to execute a bicep contraction with heavy weight really becomes a mute point if the trainer daily overlooks the client's poor core posture. Perhaps personal trainers can also borrow some yoga *asanas* (poses) themselves to incorporate into warm-ups with clients, both to improve balance and to develop isometric muscular strength at the specific angles of contractions involved. Postures like *utkatasana* and *vryksasana* develop standing posture and stability in a closed-chain exercise. For example, the former posture means sitting in a squat position from standing and holding the posture. The purpose is to teach standing alignment, balance, and strength of the core and distal muscles.

From Pilates, personal trainers can extract mindful forms of nontraditional isotonic exercise. Pilates techniques refreshingly settle the controversy about abdominal/back training placed either at the beginning or end of a session because Pilates-inspired instructors consistently challenge these core muscles *throughout* their sessions. Exercises like "hundred" and "single leg stretch" help trainers understand the importance of mindful movement and negotiation of core muscular sequencing. For example, a common exercise is to lie on one side, aligning all joints for proper alignment. The top leg abducts just an inch above the height of the top hip, and makes tiny circles in both directions from a plantarflexed position. The purpose is to teach distal stability integrated simultaneously with distal mobility, and forms an excellent core training exercise.

T'ai Chi develops not only body awareness as it relates to spatial movement, but also contributes towards balance betterment, relaxation through visualization, moving meditation abilities, and muscular control of super-slow isotonic contraction. For example, stand tall with feet together. Abduct the shoulders and bring the fingers of both hands together overhead without scapular elevation. When they touch, slowly "cover" the body, lowering the hands and elbows towards the navel. Separate the hands here, and repeat. The purpose of "sinking the chi" is to practice slow movement and relaxation, stretch the Latissimus Dorsi, and prepare for further T'ai Chi by invoking energy, or "chi" towards the body. Telling a client before a particular functional exercise (such as incline fly curls on a Resist-A-Ball©) that "today we will incorporate T'ai Chi speed in our approach to these repetitions" will change the more traditional emphasis on power and speed to one of slow control. In addition, and perhaps more importantly, it also instantly will change the mood of the workout from a "Terminator" school of fitness to a more controlled, balanced approach. Furthermore, recent research as recorded by

Ralph LaForge indicates that T'ai Chi can increase VO_2 max, balance betterment, T-Cells in those with impaired immune systems, and muscular flexibility.

Classes in Feldenkrais and Alexander Techniques can instill the benefits of slower-paced movement with closed eyes to help develop a client's inner awareness of self-movement. Traditional personal trainers follow the axim "tell, show, do" regarding explaining exercises to students. Moshe Feldenkrais was noted for the addition of his "tell, show, *imagine*, do," emphasizing that trainers should encourage clients to take a moment before an exercise to imagine themselves recruiting all of their muscle fibers in the exercise. Recent astonishing research such as printed in the *Annual meeting of the Society for Neuroscience* finds that just *imagining* muscular contraction can stimulate muscular strength. Australian born Fredrique Alexander taught his students and musicians to engage deep core musculature with eyes closed to train mindfulness, active muscle recruitment, and proprioception. The mind-body personal trainer wishing to incorporate an Alexander Technique tip will remember that the ultimate final progression challenge for any exercise shall be to perform that exercise with eyes closed. After a few successful classes incorporating some Feldenkrais and Alexander methods, no client's subsequent movement on *any* exercise with eyes closed ever will be the same again.

Guided meditation classes can teach personal trainers how to relax their clients beyond muscular flexibility. They can learn how to use the power of speech in the final moments of a mind-body personal training session, not only to emphasize the muscular flexibility component, but also to review the purposeful integration of mind and body in each and every exercise. For example, the trainer may say, "Constance, as you stretch your hamstrings sitting in this yoga staff pose, I want you to close your eyes and review with me the purpose of today, which was concentrating on the legs with mindful movement. Remember how you felt when you tried those hamstring curls, when we used the stability ball, and when we tried squats with your eyes closed." Such guided meditation helps close each training session guaranteeing your success as a mind-body personal trainer because you review what mind-body progressions you've established for your client.

Finally, aquatic mind-body classes are emerging among finer fitness facilities around the world. The water environment, often unexplored in traditional personal training classes, offers another way to complete the mission confirmed earlier of constantly adding new stimuli and variables for our clients. Personal trainers should take some mindful aquatic classes like "Hydro Yoga" or "Ai Chi" (T'ai Chi for the water). Not only will they learn strength and flexibility techniques unique to the water environment, but they will increase their success and marketability when word spreads quickly that certain trainers finish their sessions in the pool with their clients. Such aqua mind-body experiences can enrich personal trainers with such techniques as buoyancy management, balancing skills, dynamic resistance, unique flexibility skills, and relaxation techniques.

Attending such aforementioned mind-body classes benefits the personal trainer in three ways. First, the personal trainer gains an understanding of what is involved in *how* other classes at a particular facility are taught, and can thereby make a more balanced, individualized exercise prescription for the client. Second, mind-body classes can teach personal trainers different *approaches* to dealing with clients. Traditionally, a personal trainer greets a client, obtains the client's records, pats the client's back, and escorts the client towards the first exercise. Various mind-body instructors handle this encounter differently, so trainers can muster new approaches to interacting with clients. Yoga instructors, for example, tend to greet each student individually with a sincere 'hello' or 'namaste' at the door. This Sanskrit word denotes "hello" and "goodbye," and connotes "my inner peace meets, greets, and salutes your inner light." Third, when attending mind-body classes, often personal trainers can learn different exercises all together.

The acronym **N-A-M-A-S-T-E** can help the Mind-Body Personal Trainer-To-Be implement some mindful training techniques immediately without having to feel uncomfortable. The **N** stands for *nurturing* the training of the client's brain-body-breath connection. Nurturing often commences when the trainer just asks clients, not only how they are feeling in terms of body ("How's your energy level today?), but also in terms of brain and breath as well, such as "How's your concentration level today?" and "How's your breathing been this week?" Trainers can recommend reading materials. Students should be encouraged to read at least one mind-body approach article for every traditional strength training article they choose, and Mind-Body Personal Trainers may wish to begin a library of copyright-approved handouts so they can end sessions by giving their clients mind-body reading material pertinent to the day's goals. Imagine a young athlete who has trained diligently with a few, slow repetitions of heavy weight on chest and back flexors and extensors. After his session, his trainer offers a copyright-authorized article describing the benefits of meditation, with a highlighted list of local meditation classes attached. In this way, the "homework" of a mind-body class could be to take away and develop a solution to the day's mind puzzle or riddle, or a positive story or quotation. The bodybuilder receiving an article on the benefits of a yoga program during a day of rest serves as yet another example. While this approach may at first seem surprising, it will help our clients realize that we want to promote the well-being of their brain, body, and breath, thus encouraging a well-rounded approach to all parts of fitness.

The **A** stands for *aligning* the body with both mindful concentration (the brain) and breathing. Perhaps we can greet clients with something that will work their mind, such as posing a fitness fact, quiz, or riddle that may be appropriate to the tasks to be accomplished during the session. The solution can be either figured out along the way, or given at the end. Merely invoking a thoughtful quotation or a motivating story before a workout can do much to inspire one's mind and spirit also.

The **M** stands for *motivating* clients to pursue their integration of brain, body, and breath. An ultimate goal of Mind-Body Personal trainers should be to plant the seeds of motivation so that their participants pursue mind-body fitness and integration on their own. Clients should be shown the benefits of cross-training, and of cross-training the mind and spirit at that. Trainers can use clippings from the media and Internet that show how mind-body fitness is helping to round out the total approach to well being. Involving clients in new, ongoing research if appropriate, or at least including them in the latest results that become available, builds encouragement. Many motivational books like the *Chicken Soup for the Soul* series serve as excellent sources of motivational stories of people who have overcome many types of physical limitations to embrace fitness successfully.

Personal trainers with regular clients may wish to hold weekly "joint sessions" in which all clients are invited communally to a mind-body class or similar event that the trainer also attends. Perhaps the trainer and a local yoga instructor plan a special event on the last Friday of each month in which they integrate exercises for strength training with yoga asanas for flexibility training. This not only boosts motivation to take more classes and increase muscular strength and flexibility, but it also creates a boosted individual mind-body awareness and a sense of camaraderie so that members become motivated communally as well as individually. It shows how much the personal trainer cares about the holistic approach to fitness. Granted, the trainer may make no money during that hour, but the personal interest he or she shows towards client's overall health has goals that are much more far-reaching towards client accrual and retention. The buzz generated from such special events for new and former clients, truly, *will* serve as job security.

The second **A** stands for ***appraising*** the client's integration of brain, body, and breath. Trainers may wish to try to keep files on clients' feelings as well as their numerical measurements, and track these

160

over time in an interest to see emotional progress related to fitness level. For example, instead of merely "weighing in" the client and tracking measurements, record a few adjectives to describe how he or she feels regarding energy, concentration, and breathing. Watch how these change over time, and share the journey with the client periodically to note changes.

The **S** stands for *starting* sessions. Think about beginning your personal training session with the words "namaste," thereby invoking hundreds of years of mindful greeting between teacher and student. Starting sessions with a mind-body approach also means asking the client how he or she feels in terms of energy, emotions, and breath.

T stands for *transitioning.* This refers to how trainers spend their time with clients moving between and among exercises and equipment. As personal trainers become more familiar with mind-body exercises, they can begin incorporating these exercises as transitions between more traditional machine repetitions. As prudent trainers dedicate some amount of time in each session to flexibility, drawing from yoga or T'ai Chi to address flexibility proves an effective, and simultaneously innovative, way to achieve the same purpose, only in a more mindful way. For example, after a super or giant set of exercises involving abdominal flexion and other core work, having the client in some variation of the yoga "bow" posture can work wonders to open the humerus, chest, abdominal, and hip areas. Furthermore, in-between abdominal crunches on the ball and spinal extension exercises on a machine, the personal trainer could invoke the yoga postures of "cat" and "cow," calling them by these yoga names. Another option is to inject a standing yoga "tree" position between the exercises to use these muscles isometrically. Still another option is to have the client walk from one exercise to another in "bow steps," traditional, slow steps from the martial art of T'ai Chi, while concentrating on the neutral spine involved in both of the exercises targeted.

Clients love such exercises because they are not only stretching after working hard, but also feel like they're getting "more," a bit of "extra" mindfulness.

Our final letter, **E**, stands for *ending*. Mind-Body Personal Trainers should finish each session concluding the mindful journey for that day. Saying "namaste," adding guided meditation, ending a session with flexibility exercises in a pool, offering mindful reading material or handouts of brainteasers, all serve as examples of what mind-body trainers are doing. Some trainers offer green tea to their clients after training sessions. While a minor investment, recent research shows how beneficial decaffeinated or natural green tea can be as a closure to such events. Because the beverage is hot, clients must take a pause as they drink, and such pause can invite reflection, especially when coupled with a motivating handout from the trainer. Furthermore, studies by Quinlan and others have shown how beverages like green tea also help stimulate the body's relaxation process. In planning how sessions will end, trainers wishing to incorporate mindfulness must remember that the most effective session between personal trainer and client is one after which a client remembers how he or she has trained, not only the body, but the mind and spirit as well.

Developing a mind-body mission statement can help personal trainers hone their skills at making the transition to a mind-body personal coach. Since mission statements help show a congruence between what trainers hope to accomplish and actually accomplish, a mind-body mission statement will help direct the planning of their sessions to include mind and body. For example, mind-body personal trainer Deborah Puskarich of the Cooper Institute in Dallas uses the following mind-body mission statement: "to help others explore their inside power to maximize their outer potential through mindful fitness, realistic nutritional approaches, and play-related practice."

Traditionally, personal trainers tend to use the confines of the inside physical space of the confining fitness facility. If a client spends most of his or her day sitting at work prior to training, only to be led from machine to machine with his or her trainer, the latter most likely is doing an excellent job at training the former in sitting! While most clients feel that rush of excitement during lifting weights, that feeling does not last long. Adrenaline is a strong drug, but both acts and passes quickly. To keep clients in that happy, energized phase for hours after weightlifting, trainers should consider the role of serotonin.

Natural sunlight enhances serotonin production in the body, so trainers able to incorporate the outdoors can enhance overall feelings of wellbeing. To be sure, trainers must check with their legal department of respective facilities to ensure that taking clients outdoors is allowed.

Private space encouraging mindfulness

This approach includes showing clients how to achieve their realistic goals through programs that allow them to grow successfully, both by working *in* as well as in working *out*.

FOR ALL FITNESS PROFESSIONALS: WEB WISDOM

The Internet continues to change fitness and wellness drastically from the last century until now. One of the most ubiquitous and easy-to-access resources for fitness professionals today is the World Wide Web. Paradoxically, given the hectic schedules of fitness trainers and instructors, the last thing we seem to have time to do is "surf the web" for the latest in fitness information that actually can improve our productivity on a daily basis. The plethora of sites out there can prove daunting to the unseasoned internet traveler.

Perhaps the most unique aspect of the World Wide Web is that it does exactly what it claims: it gathers all of us across the globe who are involved in fitness and wellness in various capacities and unites us instantly on one computer screen. Some such sites compile a cross-section of fitness on the planet and promote a feeling of global connectivity. Ihrsa.org connects individuals to clubs all around the world, and allows IHRSA members to request guest passes to other IHRSA clubs across the planet when members travel. The site also reports on global fitness trends and statistics based on what their international clubs report.

ECAworldfitness.com has a "community" button which promotes a global consciousness for fitness professionals today, touching on topics such as specific steps fitness professionals today can take to go green as part of an environmentally-conscious community. Fitness.gov lists a calendar for every day of the year so those making fitness calendars can get ideas to implement special events and awareness at their local club, such as listing the day for national tree planting, AIDS awareness, walking, and breast cancer, for example.

IDEAfit.com offers a sense of global connectivity on their website with blogs, photos, and announcements, offering information on different ways to "inspire the world to fitness" at many of their international events. Finally, scwfitness.com has a new online magazine called "Fitness Edge" with articles and interviews from fitness celebrities in all arenas of fitness.

In addition to sites that post global trends and techniques, there are also sites that create virtual fitness communities. Fitizens.com, fitfiend.com, personaltrainernetwork.com, onlinehealthclub.com (UK), mindbodyonline.com, and fitnessnetwork.com.au (Australia) all offer valid paths to stay connected to the business side of things with those doing what you do all around the world. Most of these sites offer areas like myspace.com and facebook.com for building a fitness webpage based around your specific profiles.

In addition to building a sense of fitness community, the Internet also offers fitness professionals resources for getting practical information of movement in mostly all disciplines. Resistaball.com offers free choreography for stability ball trainers. Ptonthenet.com offers research and moves for a point-based fee which accumulate rewards like frequent flyer programs. Drlenkravitz.com offers a plethora of research on current controversies under "publications" on his site, on which Dr. Kravitz has been granting free access to all of his fitness research and published articles since 1992. A similar site, tinajuanfitness.info offers specific answers to common questions in nomenclature that everyone can use, with diagrams and permission for reprinting. Personal trainers may wish to consult pdr.com to better understand their clients Par-Q forms regarding medical terms and medicines. When a client lists regular usage of sildenafil citrate, for example, a trainer can quickly identify the drug commonly known as "Viagra."

Mind-body enthusiasts can also sharpen their chakras online. Yogasite.com and namasteinteractive.com offer a wide variety of information in impressively-easy formats to assist the yoga professional. Pilates enthusiasts can research standards at pilatesmethodalliance.com. Gyrokinesis® information exists on gyrotonic.com, NIA information appears at the impressive nianow.com, and Feldenkrais support and education exists at feldenkraisinstitute.org.

Mindbodyonline.com is an entire management resource for today's mind-body professional with different packages for sale, each allowing different levels of access to the site. Inneridea.com offers research-based articles on the most popular forms of mindful movement, with printable handouts for class distribution as well.

Most of us train special populations to some degree. For kids fitness, strongkid.com offers both research and moves for this population. For seniors (whom I prefer to call "the chronologically enriched"), unbeatable is the Canadian-based International Council on Active Aging, found at icaa.cc. This site offers a generous abundance of useful information for free. Aquatic fitness enthusiasts can join aeawave.com for resources on the liquid fitness environment. One instructor who targets this market successfully is Canadian Patricia Sawchuk (patri.fit@tele2.it), based in northern Italy. She has been successfully running her program "No Age Fitness" to this population for many years with a successful following.

For nutrition information that provides easy to understand breakdowns of what can sometimes be complicated nutritional formulas put into simple vernacular, eatright.org, caloriesperhour.com, and adairfit.com offer easy solutions. Fitday.com offers a free meal journal for clients to keep a running total of their nutrients. After spending some time at the initial setup, subsequent visits to enter food information take less and less time. An impressive service of the site is that, not only does it compile information on food trends for clients, but also lets them email their information to a trainer or nutritionist, for example. Most nutrition websites offer sections to which we can refer our clients to keep detailed meal plan diaries, and the website calculates, tabulates, and evaluates this information instantly. One additional nutritional resource, mypyramid.gov is interesting in that, not only does it offer the updated food guide pyramid, but it offers the pyramid for different populations as well, including a pyramid for Mexicans, vegetarians, and pregnant women, among others.

For the land or aquatic professional in need of supplies of any kind, power-systems.com not only serves as a one-stop shop for all products related to fitness, but also provides under "educational resources" many free articles and links on its site for further instruction about the use of those very products. They also offer a complete line of instructional dvds and books for purchase.

Sometimes the products available in today's growing fitness market can prove daunting, even to the seasoned fitness professional. Quackwatch.org is a nonprofit organization dedicated to compiling information on what's available and putting it into common terms so that everyone can decide alone. Infomercialratings.com can help fitness professionals gain more opinions to better decide on whether the products and promotions seen on television can be valid fitness resources for clients.

Given today's instant-gratification technology available with instant downloads, almost any type of information is available without the shipping expenses of the past. Group instructors can get a quick fix for moves at turnstep.com, which offers free choreography for many different disciplines. By way of caveat, just know that a potential disadvantage is that this choreography can come from anyone, and there is no standard that proofs what gets posted. Jumpybumpy.com from Britain offers peer-reviewed choreography from industry classic celebrities like Rebecca Small and Rob Glick with choices from 3-minute downloadable "combinations" (which are instantly viewable) to entire DVD downloads, to even online courses for credit. Some sites are designed for both consumers and fitness professionals in language and levels for everyone. Fitwisetraining.com allows people to design custom workouts and routines for about three dollars per move, and first-timers always get free trials.

Not all websites for fitness professionals at first glance have to do with fitness; some sites can boost business and increase productivity. Vistaprint.com offers free business cards plus the nominal charge of shipping. Spa-addicts.com and spaconnection.com link fitness professionals to luxury hotels and spas around the world. Interested professionals who want to work just a few hours a day in exchange for a complete stay (usually at top locations) should start here. Making almost any purchase from any site by first connecting to mypoints.com will allow you to accumulate points quickly that can be used towards further merchandise.

Given today's interest in training the mind as well as the body and spirit of clients, many sites offer resources for mental sharpness training for our clients. 6seconds.org, brainmap.com, implicit.harvard.edu, opencenter.org, and brainage.com all are dedicated to sharpening the major tasks of the brain in the fitness approach of exercises to be repeated. These tasks are: short and long term memory, executive and social functions, spatial, language, and math skills. At these sites, some exercises are available for a fee, some are sold, and some work in conjunction with specific hardware such as iPods and PDAs.

Are you in charge of some form of fitness schedule? You can glean ideas about your own program when you study those of others. Benefits of looking at other schedules include being able to:

- compare how others both name and describe their classes
- find out what trends exist where
- see trends in class duration

- learn who charges extra for which classes and who does not
- find out where aqua programs are thriving
- read both how personal trainers are marketed, sold, and the prices they charge
- just stimulate your own creativity by seeing what is hot around the world

Spending just thirty minutes twice per year surfing the following sites will put your finger on the pulse of trailblazing, successful, and effective programming around the world: equinoxfitness.com, thesportsclubla.com, 24hourfitness.com, holmesplace.com, goldendoorspa.com, canyonranch.com, fitnessfirst.com, goldsgym.com, and lifetimefitness.com. On these sites, be sure to click on their international links when available to experience international trends as well.

Certifying bodies have respectable sites with information, usually reserved for those who have logins provided with certifications. Afaa.com, acefitness.org, acsm.org, and nasm.org are among a few of the most popular organizations that offer both group and personal training certifications.

Today's Internet offers a wide variety of sites that can assist today's fitness professional in developing skills, seeking out continuing education, and networking in thfe industry. Setting aside just a small amount of time on a regular basis to check some of the sites listed above can help professionals stay on top of trends and take advantage of the vast array of information now available online. It was not too long ago that to seek out just half of the information available on the Internet today, one had to drive to a library and spend hours referencing different resources, which oftentimes proved unavailable after all. Today's Internet helps the fitness professional offer a more complete service than ever before with the vast amount of resources made instantly available with a few keystrokes. I wish you happy Internet surfing!

FOR MANAGERS:

MANAGEMENT OF CREAM: WE'RE ALL ON THE SAME CREAM

For cream to rise, it has to be managed with excellence. While this is primarily not a book on managing group fitness and personal training, I include some helpful suggestions for the hiring and managing. With the presence of truly an A-list cast, the responsibility heightens for their management. Since a cream staff deserves to be managed by cream managers, I include here some top tips for managing fitness staff:

1. Manager for a day

Staff can better appreciate the roles that managers have when they are given the manager's responsibilities, even if only temporarily. Both group instructors and personal trainers alike should have the privilege once per year to "walk a mile" and see the bigger fitness picture through different eyes. This generates respect and appreciation for the job that cannot be addressed in the same manner in any training; there is no substitute for walking around a facility seeing every aspect of your department through responsible eyes.

2. Praise, reward, praise

When managers have cream trainers, they have the responsibility to praise and reward them. This should be a. often, and b. in public. Too often, we hear when classes go awry, but we don't often praise our staff for work done well on a regular basis. Not all praise needs to be rewarded with money; sincere thoughts, chocolates, certificates, discount cards, pictures posted on bulletin boards, and emails and telephone class all can make staff feel rewarded.

3. Bilateral evaluations

Whenever a manager evaluates an instructor or trainer, the same opportunity should be offered of the staff member to evaluate the evaluator. When evaluations are bilateral, everyone has the chance to grow by learning where strengths and weaknesses exist. The group fitness manager evaluation I created for group fitness instructors appears in the Glossary of *AFAA's Theory and Practice* textbook. A copy of the group and personal trainer manager evaluation that I created for my staff to use while evaluating me at the Golden Door Spa in Puerto Rico since 1989 appears on the following page:

Group Exercise Manager Evaluation

Please fill out this survey at your earliest convenience. Evaluations are only effective if they work two ways, so I encourage you to help me be an effective manager to you so I can continue to empower you and provide the tools you need.

Name:

1-5 Ratings:

I rate my manager on the following scale between 1-5 where 5 is the HIGHEST SCORE for each of the following categories:

1. Overall **organization** each month of schedule (in advance, accuracy...)
   O1   O2   3O   4O   5O

2. Overall **organization of instructor communication** (phone, email, messages...)
   O1   O2   3O   4O   5O

3. Overall **quality of information** included in monthly mailings (useful information?)
   O1   O2   3O   4O   5O

4. Overall **availability** of manager (phone, email, responding to your needs)
   O1   O2   3O   4O   5O

5. Overall **customer service** of manager to you
   O1   O2   3O   4O   5O

6. Overall **ability to listen** to you and try to meet your needs
   O1   O2   3O   4O   5O

7. Overall **competency** of manager at her/his job as Group Exercise Manager
   O1   O2   3O   4O   5O

8. Overall **competency** of manager as Group Exercise **Instructor** (when applicable)
   O1   O2   3O   4O   5O

9. Overall **fairness** of Group Exercise **Manager**
   O1   O2   3O   4O   5O

10. Overall **value** of trainings manager provides for you
    O1   O2   3O   4O   5O

These are the things that I like **MOST** about working for you:

These are the things that I like **LEAST** about working for you:

The following are just SUGGESTIONS to help get you thinking how to cue the SAME response with DIFFERENT words (as a response to exercises proposed in earlier sections):

1. "engage your abs"	*"Bring your navel closer to spine." "If you are a 50 inch waist, try to squeeze in and make it a 49 inch waste." "Imagine you have a lemon behind your belly button, and squeezing it against your back muscles, make lemonade." Pilates: "brace." Yoga: "activate the uddiyana bandha." T'ai Chi: "bring the lower dan'tien closer to the ming-mong." "Hold your nose, close your mouth, and blow out to feel the transverses abdominus muscles contracting." "Shrink your wasteline."*
2. "beginner, intermediate, advanced"	*Beginner: new-to-fitness or first timer, Intermediate: someone who wants to try a more challenging version, a harder version, a moderate intensity Advanced: athlete, fitness superstar version, most challenging progression of an exercise*
3. "don't hold your breath"	*"Keep breathing" "Use your prana to assist you." "Harken to your breath." Align yourself with your breath." "Train your breath as well." "Steady your breath."*
4. "keep your spine straight"	*"Keep your spine neutral, extended, tall, lengthened, long & strong, proud, neutral, lifted, elongated"*
5. "go!"	*"I invite you to begin!" "Let's start the movement." "Begin!" "I want you to start N-O-W."*

6. "contract your pelvic floor"	*"Think about the muscles that control elimination of liquids from the front and solids from the back; now contract and close them." "No peeing in the pool" "Zip up the muscles you can control deep between your legs all the way up to the belly button." "Think about stopping urination and defecation in this movement." "Activate the muscles you use with Kegel exercises." Men: "imagine you are looking at yourself nude in a mirror and lift the testicles." Women: "imagine the muscles you would use if a tampon were slipping." "If you were in an airport running for a plane with too much coffee and diarrhea, what would you have to contract so you could still run and make your flight?"*
7. "show me good posture"	*"Stand up really __(see #4)__. Imagine that your toes, knees, hip bones, shoulders, and eyes are headlines on a car and shine all of the lights in the same direction." "Stand up like a rockstar." "Imagine that your pelvis is a bucket of water: fill it to the top and balance it."*
8. "shoulders back and down"	*"You are in the shower with ice cold water running down your back; what would you do?" "Put the shoulder blades in the back pockets of your jeans." "Show me your chest." "Open up the front of the body." "Open the heart chakra/heartspace."*
9. "squeeze!"	*"connect, contract, and compress." "Think of your muscle as a sponge full of water and contract the*

	muscle to get out all of the water." *"Concentrate on using every fiber of your being to contract this particular bodypart."*
10. "Come on! Turn it up!"	*"Let's begin!" "Here we go, team!" "Work it out!" "Show it to me!" "Make me believe it!" "Make this worth it!" "Is that all of the energy/intensity you have for me today?"*

FOR NEW GROUP INSTRUCTORS: BASIC MOVEMENT SKILLS: FROM THE PAGE TO THE STAGE

Never before have so many cardiovascular options existed for today's group fitness professional. Websites, books, and conferences all offer information on the "newer and better" advancements in both classes and equipment. Oftentimes overlooked, however, are the new instructor and low impact conditioning, a place where so many of us in the industry began. To be sure, the newer formats and equipment offerings bring excitement and cross training to fitness, but a fresh look at the often forgotten format of low impact techniques can refresh our classes.

RESOURCES

Today's new instructor often asks of other professionals "Okay, I got my AFAA certification. Now what?" Unfortunately, many international professional continuing education conferences offer courses that "preach to the choir," offering the already-seasoned instructors complex ideas using new, emerging equipment. Oftentimes, the new instructor finds little place at such conventions, and simply has to "learn the ropes" daily in the clubs by teaching and taking classes. By industry demand, however, a growing number of professional continuing education certifications now offer tracks just for the newer instructor and personal trainer. SCW (scwfitness.com) and

IDEA (ideafit.com), for example, hold "fundamentals" tracks to offer the basics of group fitness and low impact aerobics to newer professionals in those markets.

LOW IMPACT: MOVES & MUSIC

Newly-certified professionals in group fitness typically follow the format of the AFAA Primary, teaching classes consisting of mixed-impact cardiovascular conditioning, followed by a muscular strength/resistance segment without equipment. Usually, the newer instructor's classes consist of moves and music. This lack of equipment leaves the instructor with just moves and music. Truly, the technique of low impact aerobics continues to stand the test of time because of its ease, its lack of equipment, and its universality. The Aerobics and Fitness Association *Theory and Practice* text states that LIA (low impact aerobics) is "a form of exercise in which all of the movement patterns are performed with at least one foot in contact with the floor at all times. By keeping one foot grounded, the amount of stress associated with the floor impact is significantly lessened (Gladwin, 413)." Many instructors find that low impact techniques attract more people of varied ages. Patricia Sawchuk, veteran instructor based in Bergamo, Italy, has been teaching low impact conditioning for several decades. "My ladies love the benefits," she says, "because they keep not-so-youthful joints well oiled, allow us to work up a much desired healthy

181

sweat, and the choreography helps sweep the cobwebs from our brains."

One of the truest tests of the efficacy of an instructor is how well he or she can move a room with no equipment. Spending time mastering the initial basics of low impact aerobics will assist you, not only in honing your skills for this specific type of class, but also with teaching a plethora of other classes in the future involving movement to music. The basics are always the same, and to these we now turn.

BASE MOVES

Manuel Velázquez, Lead Instructor of the Golden Door Spa in Puerto Rico, believes that starting with the base moves is always the most important to start a pattern in motion. "That's what you have to plan in advance," he says, "so that you can add and layer later." Figure 1 illustrates the most common low impact techniques. With careful attention to music and cueing, just combining these elements alone easily could fill a class of any duration.

The D.R.I.L.L. Method

Instructors and guests alike, however, often seek change. Layering different elements to the base moves create the fun, diversion, and complexity of low impact classes. Sara Kooperman, CEO of SCW Fitness, uses the "d.r.i.l.l.' technique to add these layers. "I only add one of these elements at a time," she begins," to maintain a cohesiveness of the class so that everyone always feels successful. Changing more than one 'd.r.i.l.l.' element at a time could render too confusing." Figure 2 illustrates these layering options.

SAMPLES
PUTTING THE PATTERNS ON THE PAGE
A winning thirty-two count combination for low impact serves two purposes; it can both work in the warm-up at a lower intensity, and then evolve at a higher intensity in the body of the cardiovascular conditioning phase of class by layering the "d.r.i.l.l." elements.

Please consider the following example:

"Warm Up Combination"

A	RLL: March in place	1-8
B	RLL: 4 Alternating Knee Lifts stepping with the RLL	9-16
C	RLL: 4 Step touches stepping with the RLL	17-24
D	RLL: 4 Alternating Hamstring Curls with "single, single, double" rhythm	25-32

Repeat LLL

Notice the complete nature of the written choreography. The combination *name* easily identifies the purpose of the combination and will assist later with memory recall. Notice, too, that each *skill* has its separate line, indicated by a specific letter of the alphabet. Written choreography should always indicate which *lead* initiates the movement: the "RLL" signifies "right lead leg," and "LLL" signifies "left lead leg" respectively. For example, for a knee-lift involving the left knee, actually it is the right foot lead that steps to initiate that movement. The movements of lines A through D begin with the RLL. Line D itself serves as the "transition," which means that it leaves you ready to repeat the entire alphabet on the other lead for muscular balance. Finally, notice how the last column of the choreography gives a list of the actual *counts* of the movements. Knowing exactly how many counts it should take to execute a skill makes remembering a skill easier. Together, the thirty-two counts of balanced, reversible choreography become one "block."

ADDING ON

One of the most common and easy methods of teaching combinations is to use the "add-on" and "layering" techniques. For the "Warm Up Combination" above, starting the class with skill D until the class moves with great cohesiveness is appropriate because it is a balanced skill. Rebecca Small, international fitness celebrity and star of JumpyBumpy.com dvd low impact downloads, says "Of course, starting a combination with the transition skill, regardless of where it actually appears in the final combination, will make the class biomechanically and muscularly balanced from the start." There is no magic number for the time it should take; the room should demonstrate success before an instructor moves on to add on additional skills. After adding the skills A, B, and C, the combination cycles itself through with ease.

At the end of this warm up's gradual raise in intensity, the AFAA recommendation of a combination of rhythmic limbering and dynamic + static stretching is appropriate, followed by the body of the cardiovascular conditioning phase of class.

LAYERING

Many instructors become frustrated in a never ending search for new choreography. Many times, however, before searching for entirely new moves, there are techniques to freshen the current ones. The first technique is LAYERING.

The first combination of class after the warm up does not need to be an entirely new combination. In fact, since the participants are already familiar with a movement pattern, taking these same skills and applying the "d.r.i.l.l." method will help create more success and allow for creativity.

For skill A above, consider adding *direction* and *travel* the marches, taking them into a "figure 8" or large circle configuration. Adding syncopation *rhythm* is another layer of creativity, adding a pausing stomp on counts "8-7" and "4-3" when counting backwards.

For skill B, layering *travel* to the front or diagonal pattern takes the class out of its traditional movement in place. Changing the knee lifts to long-lever kicks also would increase the *intensity* while moving forward.

For skill C, adding *direction* backwards on the step-touches would return everyone to the place of beginning. Adding further *directional* change to the step-touches could take the skill into a box formation while moving backwards. Double-time *rhythm* would change the feeling of step-touches to "mini-chassés," which could be done with rhythm moving backwards or in a box formation.

Finally, layering *direction* to skill D offers options: adding half turns on the two single hamstring curls, or adding a lunge behind on the double hamstring curls, or both.

One of the most popular transition skills in low impact is the count of "single, single, double." Oftentimes overlooked, however, is the option of changing this *order,* so consider "double, single, single," and "single, double, single," as well. Play with these options!

Sometimes, complicated combinations use more than four lines and letters in which not every skill takes up eight counts of music. This advanced technique, called "split phrasing," uses movements with non-traditional counts, such as a pivot-turn mambo plus a single step touch for a total of six counts. These total combinations will still equal thirty-two counts, but with more than just four lines of eight counts each.

INVERTING

After layering, another technique to manipulate current skills involves inverting the order of skills they already know. Consider how differently the above moves would feel if you were to do the combinations on one day in this order: D, C, B, A, and, on another day B, D, A, C, for example. Furthermore, starting combinations on the LLL on some days challenges their comfort zone and helps balance their mental and physical training instead of always starting on the right foot. [space permitting: Another combination called "Grapevines" appears under Figure 3.]

Low impact conditioning can be the most versatile of cardiovascular formats because it requires no equipment, offers little impact to the body, and capitalizes on the true essence of the popularity of dance-based fitness. These techniques apply new ideas to an old format to help low impact conditioning continue to endure on our group movement schedules.

Figure 1: BASE MOVES of Low Impact Cardiovascular Conditioning, each using 2 counts minimum of music

Marches & Mambos
Step-touches
Lift steps: knees, hamstring curls, hip extensions

The "d" stands for "direction." Always begin with the simplest of directions, which is usually facing forward and in place. Next, add the *same* move facing somewhere else before actually making the step move and *travel*. Travel can occur forwards, backwards, to the sides, and on a diagonal pattern.

The "r" stands for "rhythm." These elements to explore are tempo, halftime, doubletime, and syncopation.

The "i" stands for "intensity." Popular options to increase intensity with low impact are to add arms wisely, increase the overall range of motion, and lower the body's center of gravity.

The "l.l." stand for "lever length." Longer levers increase both complexity and intensity, such as longer arms and long leg kicks.

Figure 3: Additional Combination

"Grapevines"

A	RLL: 2 V Steps with opposite arms	1-8
B	RLL: 8 Marches	9-16
C	RLL: 4 Step touches	17-24
D	RLL: Double Grapevine with a L hamstring lift on last count	25-32

Repeat LLL

POSSIBLE LAYERS to "Grapevines"
Combination:
To A add direction: first V faces front and 2nd V faces the back, making a full circle to the right
To B add direction and intensity: 4 quick chassés moving forward
To C add intensity by making them "tap-outs," side lunges with same arm overhead, and add direction traveling backwards to starting point
To D add double time rhythm to feet OR direction on a diagonal forward and back where first arrow represents first 4 counts and second represents last 4 counts

MISHAPS: WHEN THINGS GO WRONG...

There are no perfect experiences. That said, there *are* times when in fact it seems like luck is a bit more lacking than normal. The following is a list of some of the most common challenges that face instructors and personal trainers, with leading expert voices offering perhaps the world's best solutions. Instead of thinking of the following issues as "problems," if we remember that these are really "challenges" and "opportunities for growth" in disguise, we will come closer finding similar solutions to those posed here.

WHEN THE EQUIPMENT ISN'T THERE OR WHEN THERE IS NOT ENOUGH OF IT...

From Leslee Bender (benderball.com), says "when teaching a class and there are more participants than balls, possible solutions are: 1. partner up with creativity, including having one do something then have the other do something. Mindy Mylrea and I did partner play with one ball shared between us. We also incorporated Gliding disks with the partner work. 2. look for other equipment such as bands and again trade off. 3. make it a circuit with stations where they all have to do something different; each station may not include the equipment (bender balls) but emphasize something else such as cardio or flexibility. As people revolve from stations, then everyone gets to use the equipment a fair amount.

WHEN SOMEONE QUESTIONS THE VALUE OF PRE-CHOREOGRAPHED OR FREE-STYLE TEACHNG

"Being able to teach both pre-choreography programs, such as Les Mills and, free-style choreography is for a fitness instructor the best of best of both worlds. With the Les Mills programs I am able to teach to my strengths while at the same time I am motivated to hone my teaching skills in areas that I do not naturally lead with. This has definitely made me an even better instructor, coach and motivator. Teaching freestyle choreography allows me to explore my creative side and remain a versatile instructor. I have been able to take the skills I have learned in free-style and transfer them to pre-choreography and vise versa. I have been teaching group fitness for over 25 years and still loving what I do!" Maureen Hagan, 2006 IDEA Fitness Instructor of the Year and 1998 IDEA Program Director of the Year

WHEN THE MICROPHONE GOES DOWN:

From Carol Scott: "NEVER bash the club ...   roll with it.. Take the opportunity to lower the music and make it all about education. If it is a body sculpt class you can even teach without the music all together. If it is a high intensity cardio class

191

you can teach without a mike... before you begin, advise participants that due to technical difficulties, you will not be using a mike, therefore, rather than scream your head off, you will use visual cueing techniques instead so they need to pay more attention to "watching" today, than listening..

I have taught abroad never speaking and in my own classes when the mic didn't work, and it happens to be a blast! It is actually very refreshing to "shut up" for once!

Going back to speaking without a microphone... if you don't want to lower the music the entire time, select key opportunities to turn down the volume so they can hear your vocal cues. In addition, take the opportunity to "walk" the room more. Getting up close and personal with your members so they can hear you and get a more personalized experience."

FOR GROUP INSTRUCTORS:

SPECIFIC SUGGESTIONS

If you want to walk away from this book with just one or two concrete ways to make cream rise in your career, the following discipline-specific section will shed some light. NONE of these suggestions replaces the tips outlined among the pages of this book.

AQUA
- Be careful with both how and how often you break the surface of the water when you teach movement and strength. For more information on this topic, visit hydrofit.com and aeawave.com.
- Remember that in aqua fitness, you are giving exercises for 85% of the body, and 85% of the body is submersed below the surface of the water. You want to be sure that 100% of the participants are certain about what the moves should look like for this submersed 85% of the body, so teaching from the deck is only logical.

CYCLE
- Please try review cycling posture each time you ride, both for the benefit of review to those seasoned participants and the new ones.

- Try to adhere to safety suggestions of most cycling programs and keep revolutions per minute under 110 maximum.
- Always offer alternative ways to explain how to increase and decrease resistance beyond the non-specific "let's turn it up" and "let's turn it down."

HI-LO

- Unless you teach strictly a dance-based movement class, make your class "bilateral" because you are teaching movement patterns with loaded and unloaded legs. "Bilateral" means that a combination that has 32 beats of movement beginning with the right lead should be followed at some point in the class by 32 beats of movement beginning with the left lead.

KIDS

- Cammy Dennis (camjamfit@hot mail.com), FG2000 Faculty member and fitness presenter, says "My biggest pet peeve is one that has come up time and time again in the sixteen years that I've been in the arena of kid's fitness. One of the first things that people working with children need to understand is that kids are natural explorers...they use play and movement to learn about their surroundings. I often get the complaint from instructors who are new to working with kids that "they don't listen". There is this underlying assumption that most kids are naughty. I will tell you that if you invite a group of eight year olds into a fitness environment and there is a BOSU in the middle of the room, they will be drawn to it and launch themselves off of it. Understand that kids possess a very strong internal cue to discover what it is their body will experience when interacting with a BOSU (jumping, bouncing, etc.). When a baby purposefully drops their food off the edge of their high chair tray, they are demonstrating their ability to be junior scientists...they are discovering gravity. Understanding how children think will help you manage and encourage movement. Use this strong natural drive that kids possess to get them excited about moving. Channel their energy and curiosity in a positive way by making sure to maintain complete control over your environment. Harness their excitement over the activity and/or equipment you will be using. Keep your rules clear and simple. Be sure to enforce these parameters consistently.

LATIN
- Always warm up at the start and stretch at the end the *quadratum lumborum* whose role in hip movement in Latin is so crucial.

PERSONAL TRAINING
Peter Twist sheds light when he says "my second pet peeve is an era of zero academic integrity. Because trainers do not require university degrees, the awareness of the academic process from research to peer reviewed publications to professional magazines to books and onwards to the reader –the practitioner - basic academic integrity of referencing material etc is had been demolished – trainers learn in courses then copy and paste copyrighted material verbatim on their web sites and in brochures etc and gasp – in articles and in presentations too. There is a little too liberal gleaning of information – shared with the goodwill of educators; stolen and misrepresented by trainers as their own words. Even under graduate students struggle with this. It is not until graduate work that Kuhn's research methodology and academic process is taught so few in our field carry that basic courtesy and understanding with them.

I counter this pet peeve with an awareness that the world is going sedentary and most people lack the fundamental strength of character to even elevate their heart rate 20 bpm for 20 minutes without buckling to that as an intolerable challenge. So any and all trainers who are working hard to get people moving have my full support and that is why I have shared my training methods openly for 25 years. Anything that gets someone moving is a good thing. And we need motivating trainers to get the world moving. All trainers have my support – we share the same goal for people."

PILATES
- Remember that less is more with Pilates. True core control work can be exhausting with an appropriate sequence of slow-moving matwork. Adding equipment is natural when appropriate.
- An open mind is essential to practice (see YOGA). With so many Pilates schools of thought today, it's easy to fall into a trap of believing that any one way is the right way. As happens with evolution, the teachings of Joseph Pilates have evolved today, and are not what they will be tomorrow. There is space for different approaches to this discipline when they are practiced with a commitment to Joseph's Contrology. Just as you would most likely not want to visit a dentist trained in the 1940's for fillings and would want to visit a dentist updated in current research and techniques, so, too, does

197

it pay to practice Pilates with evolved research and techniques.

PRE-CHOREOGRAPHED PROGRAMMING
- The scripts and music of many pre-choreographed programming today (like lesmills.com) are so amazing they are truly fitness works of art. When you are faithful to our definition of teaching, however, you will always remember that individuals are more important than staying on script and tracks of music.

SCULPT
- Have a methodology to your sculpt class. Looking at the clock to see how much time is left and filling this time with more exercises is not a methodology. Choose equipment wisely and then decide if you are going for strength or resistance on any given day. Tell them what you've chosen, and stick with that.

STEP
- Begin every step class with a lower intensity than will develop later, like incorporating a floor mix, or by doing the very first few repeaters on the floor.
- Always begin teaching transition steps like "repeaters" and "knee lifts," regardless of where they appear in the

final combination, so that your step class is balanced from the start

- Unless you teach strictly a dance-based movement class, make your class "bilateral" because you are teaching movement patterns with loaded and unloaded legs. "Bilateral" means that a combination that has 32 beats of movement beginning with the right lead should be followed at some point in the class by 32 beats of movement beginning with the left lead.

YOGA

- When dealing with such an ancient discipline, it's best to remember that *if* yoga is about flexibility, it's about *mental* flexibility. Muscular flexibility is a by-product of practice. Regardless of how we instruct, we should remain open to other possibilities and refrain from making harsh judgments about a discipline with so many various types of practice.

SECRETS TO GREENING YOUR PRACTICE
AND YOUR FACILITY

As consumers look to personal and
group fitness instructors as role models for
planet-minded wellness, the growing concern
for the taking care of the environment
continues to form part of this responsibility.
Club managers, instructors, and trainers
alike share "going green" responsibilities of
maximizing the three greening "R"s: reduce,
reuse, and recycle. This article explores
some of the specific, immediate ways that
the fitness profession can incorporate
greening trends into daily work practice.

Figure 1 clearly shows that our planet
over-consumes its resources. World
population increase, combined with the facts
of rising global warming, an increase in the
contamination of the seas and its fish, an
increase in the concentration of acid rain,
and growing reported incidents of related
disease like asthma in children, all serve as
the canaries in the coalmine calling the
fitness environment to rise to the occasion
and make a difference.

INSIDE THE CLUB

Club managers can put their finger on
the pulse of the greening trend if they see
the fitness club through the eyes of one
making similar initiatives at his or her own
home. Of course, recycling in all
departments is the place to begin. Showers
in the locker rooms should be outfitted with
water-saving showerheads and on-demand

hot water heaters, which make instant hot water for individual showerheads and spigots. All electrical appliances throughout the facility, such as washers, driers, and computers, should be connected to smart-strips, power strips which regulate energy and reduce electrical consumption when units are turned off but still plugged in. Locker rooms and offices should be outfitted with motion sensor light switches which illuminate their respective areas only when occupied.

In the cardio-theater area, hanging televisions should be arranged to be turned on only when guests in the respective areas are using equipment. Far too often, cardio areas waste energy by having radios and televisions on with nobody in the area. Holmes Place clubs throughout Europe offer a system which provides guests the opportunity to turn on specific television sets on demand. If cardio equipment in any respective area remains deactivated for five minutes or longer, all television and sound systems in those areas automatically deactivate until turned on manually.

When laundering items like towels, choose greener brands of new "high efficiency" detergent and fabric softeners bearing the new "HE" logos (see Figure 4), and wash in cooler temperatures wherever possible. When choosing the purchase of any new electrical equipment, appliances with the new government-endorsed energy star rating logo pictured in Figure 2 will consume less energy and also decrease electrical bills. Wherever possible, replace light bulbs throughout the facility with the new "CFL" energy-saving light bulbs which feature bulbs that spiral and reduce electrical consumption.

Printing for all matter in the facility should use post-consumer recycled paper wherever possible. Electronic schedules, brochures, and descriptions displayed on the internet instead of paper printing are quickly becoming the norm for large fitness chains such as equinoxfitness.com

. For any areas that incorporate aromatherapy, water diffusers provide more environmentally friendly options than incense and scented candles by not releasing smoke and other chemicals into the environment.

Many facilities today offer food and beverage areas like juice bars and restaurants. Some greener approaches include using recycled and biodegradable material in printed matter, paper plates, and to-go packaging. Bags made of corn fibers often replace non-degradable plastic bags. Clubs show a green-minded consciousness when they offer menus including options that support the slow-food movement, locally-sourced choices, organic choices, sustainable seafood choices where appropriate, and fair-trade options for chocolate, tea, and coffee. Figure 3 lists websites offering further information on greening, and the first ten websites detail greener approaches with food.

Finally, when evaluating staff, providing "green" typed and emailed evaluations shows an environmentally-conscious focus.

PERSONAL TRAINERS

Personal trainers are perhaps the most widely viewed of all club employees on a daily basis, so they truly set visual examples on many levels. Trainers can display a green consciousness in several ways. Recycled water bottles are a better choice than purchasing bottles on a daily basis, but plastic bottles should be opaque. Clear plastic water bottles that have a color are likely to contain Biphenyl A (BPA), a chemical which leads to toxicity and can accumulate in the bloodstream. Greener choices include choices at nalgene-outdoor.com and thegreenguide.com. Most fitness professionals today tend to avoid choosing plastics altogether in favor of stainless steel bottles. Read more at thinkoutsidethebottle.org.

Trainers should take a green approach to prescribing and using fitness equipment by minimizing the use of electrical-based machine training. Since outside training tends to focus on human effort and natural light, it is perhaps the greenest approach to training for cardiovascular, flexibility, and closed-chain bodyweight exercises. When carrying personal equipment to and from the club, consider using backpacks made of recyclable material able to harness solar power to charge electrics contained within (cellphones, PDAs, laptops), available from sources such as voltaicsystems.com and noonsolar.com.

Trainers can use less paper by using personal digital assistants such as cellphones and other portable devices when tracking client progress. Not only does this approach preserve more trees, but it also allows trainers to manipulate data on a computer, including forwarding progress, follow-up, and feedback directly to client via paperless emails.

GROUP FITNESS

Music of all kinds unites almost all group fitness instructors, and serves as a significant point of departure for a green approach. Downloadable music provides instant gratification without non-green plastic cases, shrink-wrap, and even postage. Options such as dynamixmusic.com and clickmix.com allow instructors to choose their own tracks, beats per minute, and organization, only to download a complete playlist almost instantly to a computer or iPod for immediate use.

Other options exist beyond music. Mind-body instructors can choose natural, degradable mats at huggermugger.com. Ultralighttowels.com offers degradable, compact, and efficient towels for fitness instructors on the go who usually rely on using different towels at different facilities.

When washing fitness clothes at home, instructors can also exercise the same greener practices for laundry described above. Deborah Puskarich, Group Fitness Director of Dr. Kenneth Cooper's Aerobic Center at Craig Ranch, takes a greener approach to group fitness once monthly in which a class works out to no music, no lighting, and no microphone, saving on equipment wear-and-tear and electricity. Truly, the only energy generated is entirely human.

AROUND THE WORLD

Fitness facilities around the globe are making progress towards implementing greener practices. In the Philippines, Gold's Gym chains in locker rooms reduce laundry and towels by offering standing "Body Blower" machines after showers to dry clients with warm air. In Japan, Athlie fitness clubs offer parking areas only for bicycles, encouraging all guests to use bicycles and do their cardiovascular workouts coming *to* the gym instead of using cars. In the United Kingdom, a country with heavy rainfall, clubs like Virgin Active are taking after the British Airways precedent at their new Terminal 5 by capturing rainwater on the roofs which is filtered and used for their sinks, showers, and toilets. Finally, and most excitingly, in Rotterdam, "Club Watt" has developed the technology to capture the energy generated by people using electronic cardiovascular equipment like treadmills, stair steppers, elliptical machines, and even group cycling classes! Energy is routed to, and captured on, rechargeable batteries, and this in turn fuels the gym's electrical needs for the following day. Knowing that the energy from today's classes literally generates the club's energy for tomorrow creates a strong emotional connection among all of the club's guests.

The greening trend around the world has many implications for the fitness environment. The ideas above serve as just a start for implementing more environmentally self-aware aspects of fitness for managers, trainers, and instructors. If we want a truly green approach to running our fitness business--something we have never had--truly we have to start doing what we have never done.

Figure 1
Year
Approximate Population

Year	Approximate Population
1800	1 billion: the ideal sustainable ecological maximum for our planet
1930	2 billion
1960	3 billion
2008	6.4 billion

Source: Center for Disease Control, CDC.gov

Figure 2

Figure 3
- ECO-INDEXTOURISM.ORG
- FOODANDWATERWATCH.ORG
- THINKGREEN.COM
- VERIFYSUSTAINABILITY.COM
- GARDEN.ORG
- SLOWFOODUSA.ORG
- CARBONFOOTPRINT.COM
- ORGANICCONSUMERS.ORG
- FOOTPRINTNETWORK.ORG
- TREEHUGGER.COM
- ENERGYSTAR.GOV /ECO-LABEL.COM
- NATURE.ORG
- NRC-RECYCLE.ORG/LOCALRESOURCES.ASPX
- MBAYAQ.ORG./CR/SEAFOODWATCH.ASP
- CSPINET.ORG/EATINGGREEN/INDEX.HTML
- MYGREENTRAVELS.COM
- GREENGLOBE.ORG
- USGBC.ORG
- CARBONNEUTRAL.COM
- WWW.UCSUSA.ORG

Figure 4: "High Efficiency"

TO PRE-CHOREOGRAPH OR NOT: THAT IS THE QUESTION TODAY'S GROUP FITNESS INSTRUCTOR MUST DECIDE

As group fitness schedules across the globe evolve, three distinct groups of programming types emerge. The first group consists of an exclusively freestyle approach in which instructors develop their own content and descriptions for classes. The second group is situated at the other end of this continuum, and consists of the pre-choreographed approach in which instructors buy into programming that comes complete, from moves to music. The third group finds itself in the middle of these two extremes, offering instructors set templates for class organization, while granting them the freedom to fill these templates with options from among a variety of organization-approved selections. Today's instructors choose from among these three approaches, sometimes exclusively selecting one, or sometimes choosing to follow two or all three. Here, industry experts from all approaches shed some light on the advantages of these approaches.

The freestyle approach to fitness has existed for many years as countless instructors like to be exclusively responsible for, and in charge of, selecting their own moves and music. A distinct advantage to this system is that they do not have to follow anyone else's programming and can show their own creativity. A disadvantage is that such instructors, especially when they are new, lack a support system in developing their own programs.

Some freestyle instructors like the variety of change instead of following a script. June Kahn, 2009 IDEA Instructor of the Year, chooses only this freestyle approach, stating "I need the freedom to be able to change my communication techniques in class dynamics which can vary by the hour. I like to be able to interact, use their names, and make individual references and progressions as appropriate to empower them to the fullest, avoiding any possible repetitive stress syndrome from an otherwise non-changing program."

Because many instructors teach at multiple facilities, they often feel the need to reinvent their moves and music, not only to keep classes feeling fresh, but also to avoid giving the same product at the competing clubs for which they teach for marketing reasons. "If I taught the same land or aqua class all over the city," says Michele Regev of Los Angeles, California, "there would be no special reason to join my classes at a particular place because my product would be the same everywhere. We have to follow AFAA's Standards and Guidelines, while simultaneously standing out and offering unique options in this aggressive economy. Nothing is special and unique and programming that appears all over the city."

At the other end of our spectrum, the pre-choreographed approach to fitness has also existed for centuries. History shows that, in ancient Greece, trainers used some of the same movement patterns for all men regardless of their particular sport as they prepared for competitions. One size was supposed to fit all. (Perrottet) Many exercisers today can recall following a long-playing recorded routine in the last century, matching movements to music with Jane Fonda's early exercise routines, which treated everyone in the same way. Judi Sheppard Missett's program from 1969, "Jazzercise®", enjoyed tremendous success as it virtually taught pre-choreographed movement to music with a "song and chorus" approach. As popularity increased, subsequent instructors of such programs went on to memorize the programs created by the developers as the movement grew.

Today, pre-choreographed programs have evolved in many ways from those first days. In programs such as Les Mills International and Body Training Systems, instructors sign up (and pay up) to receive beautifully-produced dvds, professionally printed manuals, continuing education credits, and legal, real-artist music. An advantage to this system is that instructors do not have to develop their own music and moves for their classes. As actors learning roles, they receive a script prepared by award-winning instructors, and their task is to commit this to memory.

Chalene Johnson, CEO of Powder Blue Productions, says that "pre-choreographed programming allows instructors whose strong suit may be personality, motivation, and connecting to focus on what they do best and leave the creating, testing, and development of each class up to the experts." Lyndsay Murray-Kashoid, movement specialist based in Dallas, Texas, agrees, teaching choreographed "Core Fusion" classes at Exhale Spas. "I teach classes choreographed by someone else because I like the advantages of having a game plan for every class that is set in stone and easily marked. This gives me peace of mind so that I can focus on making every section count and keep a balance to the workout, and, for the guests, that provides an element of predictability that allows them to follow me more efficiently."

Emma Barry, Creative Director for Les Mills International, claims that pre-choreographed programming offers instructors proven, winning support. She says that, for the independent instructor, "the world is a different place because:

- You are alone
- If you are bad or new there is no system to support you to be better
- If you are good or seasoned there is nobody to replace you when you are not around
- You lack the camaraderie of like-minded people on a mission
- You may not be great at delivering the "end to end" process involved in creating and delivering a group fitness

experience - and most people aren't."

The third group of programming fuses the two approaches, giving instructors both teaching systems and room to make more choices from lists of approved content and music. Five current and successful programs of this type are "Balletone" (under Creative Director Shannon Fable), "Turbo Kick" (created by Johnson), "Latin Blaze (created by Jamie Smith)," "¡Ay Caramba! (created by Manuel Velázquez)" and "Zumba (co-created by Beto Pérez)." These five teacher trainings offer instructors templates and tools to create their own classes, including music, base moves, and pre-set choreography to get them started.

Fable says that this type of education is different from pre-choreographed programming, teaching instructors *how to create* successful choreography instead of just supplying it. "Teaching them the *why* behind the *how*," she says, "this approach creates a system by which they can teach multi-level classes without the need for everyone following the same, unchanging choreography." Joy Prouty, Zumba Education Specialist, says "we give instructors a proven template to follow and then let our instructors chose what they teach, never using more than four moves per song: $Z = M/C^2$ (Zumba = Music/Core Steps and Choreography)."

Deborah Puskarich, Group Exercise Director of Cooper Fitness Center at Craig Ranch in Dallas, Texas, accepts two of our three approaches. Although she does not teach pre-choreographed programming, in addition to being a freestyle instructor, she also teaches template programs like Zumba. "Coming up with my own step choreography is a *creative* challenge for me, and learning the Zumba program is a *learning* challenge. I never realized how much both types of challenges make me a better instructor."

Maureen Hagan of Goodlife Fitness Clubs in Canada accepts all three approaches. "I teach Les Mills because it provides me with a world class program that I, or any GoodLife instructor, can teach, making all of us as Les Mills instructors feel supported as part of a world-wide team. On the flip side, I teach template and my own freestyle classes because it gives me the opportunity to be creative as it challenges me to develop new exercises and teaching techniques. I enjoy the best of all worlds with variety in my career."

Today's instructors can be more versatile than ever before given today's expanded group class schedules. As we prepare for teaching so many different types of classes, sometimes putting preparation time into all of them does not prove possible. Johnson advocates both freestyle and pre-choreographed formats, and suggests that today's instructors try both, claiming "I think there will always be a need for the creativity of freestyle classes, but pre-choreographed workouts were a necessary evolution of our industry. For instructors who want to teach multiple, different formats, it is unrealistic to assume we have the time or the talent to master all of them. Why not let someone do the work for you in one or two of those formats that you know will be successful and flawless?"

Whichever of these three avenues an instructor today chooses, the industry offers support for all of them so each instructor can be both popular and professional. From live trainings to internet webinars, the fitness tools available to instructors today are unparalleled than ever before. As group exercise offerings today prove to be more diverse and exciting than ever, room definitely exists for all of these approaches to co-exist in harmony as instructors continue to showcase our talents.

"NOT MISTAKING THE FOREST FOR THE THREES": TRILOGIES OF FITNESS

Today's fitness professional requires an almost innate sense of numbers. From thinking and counting in terms of even numbers to grouping muscles in oppositional sets of two with agonists and antagonists, the profession seems to be one based on concepts that are dividable by two. Be that as it may, the odd number three offers several new ways to view the fitness profession via some refreshing trilogies, important wellness concepts based on three cornerstones each.

Fitness professionals have a plethora of responsibilities: from safety, to coaching, to dealing with individuals with a range of special needs and abilities. Whether reviewing safety responsibilities--like staying on top of AFAA's Basic Exercise Standards and Guidelines--or developing creative exercise programming, learning to view the profession with an eye on these "bigger picture" trilogies will help keep a refreshing outlook for classes and clients.

Trilogy #1: HOW WE MOVE
The first fitness trilogy that unites all humans is the foundation for movement itself, as depicted in figure 1.

Figure 1
   Ability + Agility

Stability   Mobility

    The words "stability," "mobility," and "ability/agility" summarize this author's conceptualization of all of group fitness from the point of view of movement specialist. "Stability" connotes the foundation of movement. From posture to preparing the setup of an exercise before adding mobility, this word summarizes the precursor of movement itself. As babies, we experiment recruiting enough motor neurons to be able to hold ourselves up in a quadruped position long before adding mobility towards crawling, hence the importance of stability before mobility. As a building is only as strong as its basement or foundation, stability acts as a determining factor for the rest of life. Improper biomechanics, postural deviations, and inappropriate exercise, and even lack of proper breathing mechanics all can lead to instability.

    The concept of *stability* not only involves proprioception and balance, but also muscular strength, endurance, ergonomics, and even controlled mobility. Stacey Lei Krauss, founder of the "willPower method," based in Colorado, agrees, stating "stability training ... in 'willPower & grace®,' addresses stability by working barefoot, requiring a recruitment of the many intrinsic muscles of the feet, which are typically supported by a shoe. If we become stronger from the ground up through our entire kinetic chain emphasizing stability first, our mobility quality will be more efficient and effective." Research tells us that stability, then, is the precursor to mobility (Bronner).

The concept of *mobility* not only involves movement, but also grace, muscular efficiency, flexibility, and even dynamic stability. Successful, pain-free movers are able to add mobility to a strong sense of what this author terms "stability validity" in order create the third point of this trilogy, ability and agility. Activities of Daily Life, called ADLs, are a combination of both abilities and agility training in some form (Wolf). Kraus says that all of her programs focus on the stability-mobility relationship as individuals develop skills to "maintain a stable core while engaging in mobility in order to control deceleration. We need to manage both our own body weight stability and our movement while gravity takes hold," says Krauss. ADLs occur, then, from the interdependence of the cornerstones of this trilogy.

"Ability" refers to our ADLs, and "agility" includes being able to react to the constantly-unexpected forces of life, like being able to avoid a swerving car when walking. According to the Surgeon General of the United States (www.surgeongeneral.gov/library/), achieving safe *ability* should be everyone's goal as everyone should strive to avoid a sedentary lifestyle.

A lack of discipline in this trilogy can yield injury. "I don't have clients claiming they got injured when they were just sitting and emailing," says AFAA Provider Jamie G. Smith of the "Latin Blaze" craze. "They get injured during *mobility* with dysfunctional body mechanics. We achieve movement by training both isometrically and isotonically because together these two methods mimic the stability and mobility of life, respectively." Training the body, then, means developing *ability* by training both the *stabilizing* and *mobilizing* systems of the body, through both isometric and isotonic training, where appropriate.

Trilogy #2: WHAT WE NEED

If our first fitness trilogy explains *how* humans move, then the next trilogy depicted in Figure 2 illustrates *what* humans need to train when they engage in movement.

Figure 2
Cardiovascular

Strength   Flexibility

Whatever one's particular niche in fitness, everyone needs to train to some degree cardiovascular, strength, and flexibility. While this may be the most easily-recognized of fitness trilogies, oftentimes it is the most imbalanced. For example, instructors of cardiovascular exercise oftentimes themselves miss out an adequate training in flexibility and strength, if for no other reason than for the fact that they spend their work time just doing cardiovascular work.

All movers interested in their own health should ask themselves what they could improve in their own training regarding this trilogy; personal trainers and instructors should advocate a complete balance in overall training to clients, perhaps by merely recommending group fitness classes that trains their weaknesses. AFAA Certification Specialist Jay Guillory, based in Houston, TX, teaches strength classes regularly and also recommends other classes. "I always remind my students not to short-change themselves by always doing what is familiar. Sometimes, the things we don't like to do are the things we need to do more of. If they enjoy my strength training, implementing a couple of days of cardio and flexibility training into their regimen would help them achieve more balanced approach to total wellness." Furthermore, training these systems with a consideration of the first trilogy also helps cross-train the body effectively; there should be aspects of stability and mobility training *within* cardiovascular, strength, and flexibility training.   Balance within this training trilogy, then, is key.

Trilogy #3: WHO WE ARE
Perhaps the most popular of fitness trilogies today involves the "mind-body-spirit" combination shown in Figure 3.

Figure 3

Body

Mind/Brain   Spirit/Breath

Although the traditional words used to describe this fitness approach are "mind, body, and spirit" fitness, these words sometimes can disconcert some individuals and cultures because of preconceptions, misinformation, and stereotypes. Perhaps more individuals would embrace the notion of mindfulness and "whole-istic" centered training if there existed less misconceptions for the word "mind," which often includes thinking that mind-body fitness includes a component of mind-altering techniques, influencing communication, or religious practices.

Lyndsay Murray-Kashoid, Yoga and Core Fusion Instructor of Exhale Spa based in Dallas, Texas, says "actually, 'mind-body-spirit' fitness really just means working within the framework of acute mindfulness, and training that mindfulness during movement to yield richer movement. The word 'mind' really refers to a strong mental component involving keen concentration on, and coordination of, the other two ends of our triangle, the breath and body." To help allay common fears, many today replace the word "mind" with "brain" to make the concept seem less threatening and more related to traditional fitness since the word "brain" denotes a more tangible, anatomical reality.

Similarly, common misconceptions for the word "spirit" include some thinking that this refers to a particular cult, sect, or particular religious organization or affiliation. In mind-body fitness, however, the word "spirit" at its most elementary level refers to an acute focus on breathing because the etymology of the word derives from the Greco-Latin words "spiritos," meaning both "breath" and "energy" (Benson). Many times where the word "spirit" would result in alienating some from the real message of "mind-body-spirit" fitness, some professionals choose to adopt the alliterative words "brain-body-breath" fitness to more convey more physically the emphasis of this trilogy. Murray-Kashoid reveals "the exerciser who only half breathes only achieves half potential."

Today, many healers and life coaches like Melissa Baumgartner, an AFAA International Specialist and Owner of Wellness Speaks, recommend both an awareness of, and training for, mind-body-spirit fitness. "Doing something each day for not only your body, but your brain and breath as well, can really improve the overall quality of your life," she says, "by keeping you grounded to the present and staying aware of what is important." Baumgartner recommends "taking time to pause throughout your day, breathe deeply, and connect with how you feel physically and emotionally." Results, she says, are better than thinking about the body alone because, "when we connect mindfulness to movemen, we carry the habit of awareness into our everyday lives. This translates to more mindful choices, or as my clients have discovered: better choices more often."

Trilogy #4: WHERE WE MOVE

The third trilogy pertains to where all movement occurs, the planes of movement.

Figure 4

Transverse   Frontal

One of the most interesting aspects of movement is how all mobility possibilities occur in only three planes of movement. Both group and private trainers often and easily fall into the easy trap of training movements in the same planes. For example, while flexion and extension always occur in the sagittal plane, the muscular *movement pattern* does not have to occur in the same plane each time. "Changing up the way I train my clients to avoid training plateaus is part of my philosophy," says Smith. "In creating change to exercise design, I try to include the planes of motion as training variables as well. For example, I may have my clients try elbow flexion repetitions with their arms out to the sides at shoulder height to add frontal plane mobility as a progression involving the deltoids as stabilizers. Similarly, I may add transverse plane rotation to clients holding a side-plank, having the upper arm reaching under and through the body in a 'thread-the-needle' fashion." Using the three planes of movement as variables in training clients, then, avoids training plateaus because different planes make the muscular system respond with different neuromuscular stimuli.

The last trilogy addresses the way fitness professionals can view training the body, separating it into upper body, lower body, and core. It is no coincidence that the AFAA Primary and Personal Fitness Trainer certification examinations address the body in this way. Helping fitness educators understand how the distal body parts (the upper and lower extremities) both connect to, and coordinate with, the proximal (the core) remains one of the most important messages of the AFAA certification process. Figure 5 represents this view.

Figure 5

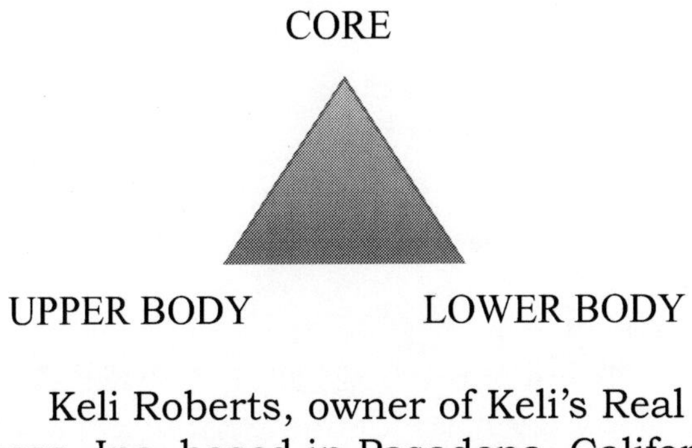

CORE

UPPER BODY   LOWER BODY

Keli Roberts, owner of Keli's Real Fitness, Inc, based in Pasadena, California, finds that sometimes dividing up training this way can be highly effective. "I like to focus on regions of the body with compound movements and exercises that target multiple muscles. For example, I teach workouts with a lower body, upper body, and core focus at Equinox. Every pattern involves triplanar movement patterns and integration with a core connection in some way, regardless which body part we are emphasizing at any one moment."

Other instructors agree that maintaining a focus on this trilogy helps keep classes functional. Valerie Nosenzo, Group Exercise Coordinator for Frito Lay based in Plano, Texas, realizes the importance of running an ever-changing group fitness schedule. "Since I have to change class names and formats often," she says, "I always start by thinking about the relationship between the upper and lower body connecting through the core when deciding if an exercise is functional or not. We avoid isolation exercises like seated biceps curls because they usually forget the core, but exercises that integrate either the upper or lower extremities with core activation keep intensity high and stay functional simultaneously." Illustration #1 shows some practical examples.

Illustration #1:
Using this trilogy as a checklist for total body exercise design, then, can serve as an additional tool for instructors asking themselves how to be sure if movements are

appropriate for a class. "Almost everything we do," says Nosenzo," is either:

- upper body plus core exercise (like plank push-ups and side planks)
- lower body plus core exercise (standing lunging wood-chops with core rotation),
- total body exercise including the core (like supine single leg bridges with shoulder pullover)."

As group fitness instructors and personal trainers strive to keep their programs fresh with classes and clients, trying to develop strategies for implementing change in an effort to train the whole person can prove challenging. Contemplating the five trilogies mentioned in this article yields at least fifteen considerations for trainers when devising change. As outlined with the figures in this article, sometimes the *odd* number three can offer much to keep the training of our clients *even*.

References:
Benson, H., & MacDonald, A. (2004). *Mind Your Heart: A Mind/Body Approach to Stress Management Exercise and Nutrition for Heart Health.* New York: Free Press.

Bronner, Brownstein. (1997). *Evaluation Treatment and Outcomes Functional Movement in Orthopedic and Sports Physical Therapy.* New York, NY: Churchill Livingstone, Inc.

Surgeongeneral.gov

Wolf, Chuck. (2001). "Moving the Body." *IDEA Personal Trainer,* June.

SMALL MAKES BIG: SMALL DETAILS THAT MAKE BIG CHANGES IN GROUP AND PT SESSIONS

DRAMA IN THE DETAILS

As group fitness instructors prepare for our classes, we put countless hours of preparation into the major components like program design, music, equipment, and practice. While these are the major, necessary aspects of the group fitness experience, there are also minor aspects of classes that make big differences in the total resulting experience for each participant. Mindy Mylrea, recipient of the 1999 IDEA International Fitness Instructor of the Year award, says "when group fitness leaders create classes that are safe and effective, that's our job. But there are *little* things that we can do to effect *big* differences, and cream rises to the top," and to those little things in the personal training and group fitness world we now turn.

THE PRE-SHOW

Setting the stage for a class or personal training session can involve introducing a special theme that pertains just to that day. Patricia Moreno, creator of SATIlife, an instructor training program based in New York City, often sets the stage before her sessions writing key words across the mirrors in the studios with large, non-permanent markers. She writes out the theme for a particular class using such words as "intensity," or "empowerment," and then references this throughout the class. Similarly, Douglas Brooks, exercise physiologist and personal trainer based in Mammoth Lakes, California, says "I often suggest that trainers give their clients a focus for every workout. Whether it be to concentrate today on 'breathing,' 'speed,' or 'balance,'" Brooks says, "they should always have one special thing that is unique for that session as a particular focus."

Kayoko Takada, owner of "Pilates Alliance" and programming director for Athlie Gyms in Tokyo, Japan, suggests arriving early when appropriate to set up the room to be able to greet the guests as they arrive, standing at the door and bowing to each one. "This gives eye contact with each person and lets everyone feel special like I have been waiting for everyone. If they have something special to tell me [like pregnancy or injuries], they feel comfortable doing so upon entering instead of having to call it out later in front of the room when everyone will hear."

SMART STARTS

Jay Blahnik, Presenter, Product/Programming Consultant and Author with over twenty-two years of experience based in Laguna Beach, California, agrees with Brooks, and always tries to incorporate education from the warm-up, stating "I am always looking for ways to provide teachable moments that provide almost invisible education, creating a focus of the day in each class. For example, in my running class, I may say 'The focus today is efficiency. Spend time during your workout today thinking about how you can be more efficient in your posture, foot strike, arm swing and breathing.' Setting the stage with a theme allows me to imbue education into any class."

DURING

The center of the session or class is where we spend the most amount of time with our clients, so demonstrating some "cream" skills in the body of class or session shows our attention to even the most minor of details in the "show" aspect.

MANIPULATING THINGS, NOT PEOPLE

During the group experience, Steve Feinberg, creator of Speedballfitness.com based in New York City, changes both the volume of music and brightness of lighting *several* times in each class. "Just as a Broadway production changes sets and moods, class should do the same. Not only do I want to dim the lights when everyone is supine, but also match the lights and volume to the intensity of the class to match the peaks and valleys."

Just as Feinberg manipulates the look and feel of a class experience, Calvin Wiley, dancer and choreographer based in New York City, manipulates the orientation of the students. Wiley oftentimes will change where the "front" of the room is in order to force students outside of their normal comfort zones. Furthermore, he often splits the room in different ways, forming both "performers" and "cheerers" watching the production as the participants run the choreography before switching their roles.

Jeffrey Bornman, celebrity trainer based in West Hollywood, California, believes that personal training sessions set themselves apart from others when they offer a client the chance to draw a connection between a condition in their life and a condition that is manifesting in their body. One tool he uses is to focus on a body part, muscle group or a specific exercise or activity that can expanded into a metaphor for life. For example, legs (which *stand under* us) can be used to represent understanding. At one point in the workout he may say "This is just like life; being strong is important, but it takes flexibility in our understanding (legs) to use our strength most effectively. Invariably," he says, "clients come to a future session excited to share a realization they had "after thinking about our legs discussion last week." "
Bornman shows that simple, costless tools can imbue additional value into personal training sessions.

These examples of group dynamics show how instructors and trainers can manipulate the sights, sounds, and feel of class and session dynamics.

SMART IS ATTRACTIVE

Keli Roberts, recipient of the 2003 IDEA International Instructor of the Year award, based in California, weaves science into her workouts. Uniquely known for studying research about the strength routines she teaches before creating them, Keli creates intense workouts people love. Her ability to fuse that science-based information into the classes she teaches while making people sweat is uncanny. She says "first, I study research first to know how to maximize benefits and minimize time, and then I practice a lot before taking that preparation to classes. When I teach, I try to explain *why* we are doing a particular sequence so people understand that they're not just moves, but moves based on science-proven information."

Interjecting theory into practice proves to be a sign of many of the industry's great teachers and trainers. Pilates master June Kahn, recipient of the 2009 IDEA International Fitness Instructor of the Year award, based in Colorado, weaves the original eight concepts of Joseph Pilates into every experience she creates. "The principles are not meant to be something we learn and then forget about," she states, "because a really effective instructor uses each principle in two ways. First, an instructor can bring *any* of Joe's principles into play at any time, in any Pilates progression, and apply it to the work. Second, a really good instructor can relate that same principle metaphorically to something in life and transcend the experience of just being on the mat. I relate the principle of 'balance,' for example, to many things like posture, moderation, and kinesthetic awareness.

POWERFUL IS PRACTICAL

Outstanding teachers and trainers know the value of teaching to their clients, not at them. Instead of trying to sound erudite, they discover ways to make their clients *feel* education instead of just *hearing* it.

Shannon Fable, Fitness Author, Consultant, Manager and Program Developer based in Colorado, knows the value of relating to the people in the room. "Knowing your students is imperative," she says, "because each person is an individual with a unique reality that is looking to YOU to make them feel successful. It's a tall order, but getting to know your people is crucial in helping meet their expectations."

Dominique Adair, Director of Adair Fitness and Nutrition, Los Angeles and New York based consulting company, knows that one of the pitfalls of discussing nutrition with private clients is that too much time is spent time focusing on numbers, calculations, and grams. "People leave understanding math but not understanding what kinds of food make healthy choices," she adds. To help solve that kinesthetically, she schedules practical time in grocery stores with her clients. Walking by specific samples of raw, macrobiotic, organic, and local foods, she lets people see and taste what they are discussing in order to learn how to make healthy choices independently. "This allows my clients to learn how to think for themselves to make healthful choices," she says.

ENDINGS

The last minutes of a personal training session or class are as important as the first five minutes because these are the moments that people will take away. Maybe deviations from the original plans occur in the class body to accommodate the actual abilities of the participants, but, like the warm-up, the ending can be scripted and rehearsed.

Petra Kolber, recipient of the 2001 IDEA International Fitness Instructor of the Year award and spokesperson for Yes! Fitness Music, based in Redondo Beach, California, says "the start and finish has to be prepared and polished because these are the 'lasting impressions' that people will remember." Petra also believes that the beginning of class actually starts from the "pre-show, the moment you step foot inside the gym. How you treat everyone you come into contact with as you make your way into the studio or onto the gym floor will tell the people around you a lot about what they can expect from you as an instructor, trainer and human being."

Leslee Bender, creator of the Bender Academy of Training based in Reno, Nevada, teaches evolved, science-based Pilates movements with and without equipment. During her classes and workshops, participants learn different levels of exercises, which she calls "selective stabilization." The magic occurs in the ends of her classes, however, when she plays a special song and weaves all of the moves learned thus far into one graceful, but unexpected, production song. Bender makes class seem like disconnected movements until the surprising final flow.

Lisa Wheeler, National Creative Manager for Group Fitness at Equinox, based in New York City, does the same with Broadway-influenced dance-based movement. During class, participants think they are learning blocks of choreography until she reveals the Broadway show in the final five minutes from which the choreography derives, and even more excitement ensues.

Whether we study the pre-show, the start, body, or endings of our sessions, putting thought and preparation into the small details outlined here by some of the industry's great teachers and trainers will help set ourselves apart from the rest in today's competitive market. Ultimately, cream rises to the top when we prepare and polish as many aspects of our craft as possible, including these often ignored details of the experience.

SELF CARE FOR TODAY'S TRAINERS:
IF YOU DON'T TAKE CARE OF YOUR
SENSES, THEY CAN'T POSSIBLY TAKE
CARE OF YOU!

In today's unique economy, group
fitness instructors oftentimes need to be as
versatile as possible in an effort to make
financial ends meet. Sparse are the true
"full time positions" with benefits for
instructors, and far more common are the
instructors that teach in multiple facilities.
Be that as it may, the propensity for today's
instructors to face overtraining symptoms
looms higher than ever. To that end, a few
homework tips to avoid burnout and
promote career longevity always serve as
welcome gifts for instructors, forming a "spa
for the soul."
A unique, new buzzword of this
century is "self-care." This refers to putting
the necessary parameters in place to ensure
that our career machine, the body which
takes so much abuse from class to class,
receives routine maintenance and service.
Examples of such overwork abound: from
teaching in facilities with no microphones
and less than ideal acoustics, to teaching in
facilities with improper temperature control,
to having to over-teach in an effort to meet
financial requirements, and even to self-pay
medical benefits or even exist without them.
Proper instructor self-care encompasses
treats for the five senses. The acronym

"V.E.E.T.S." outlines practical steps instructors can take.

"Self-care" means promoting both the relaxation response and recovery. When we live in stress, the *sympathetic* nervous system keeps us active. Called the "fight or flight" syndrome, this is the nervous system that keeps us on our toes when we teach and train. Unfortunately, it is also the system that keeps us in stress and dis-ease. Conversely, the body's ability to heal itself consists of the *parasympathetic* nervous system, and this turns on when we put attention into any of the little exercises outlined in this article.

V is for VOICE (and TASTE)

Avoiding vocal overuse proves impossible in our industry. Nevertheless, taking care of one's voice is paramount to health so that proper curing will be possible. First, prudent clubs provide microphones for all teaching environments, especially where sound tends to be an issue and acoustics are less than ideal. Cycle rooms, pools, and group fitness rooms figure among the most common examples. With a microphone, be sure to adjust the volume accordingly so that the spoken (not shouted) word is sufficient. Second, when using the voice without a microphone, be sure to project from the diaphragm, and trying to lower one's voice assists with this projection. As instructors teach, the sympathetic nervous system often dominates, and voices tend to rise in both volume and pitch. Instead, remembering to project with a lower than normal pitch when teaching assists in maintaining vocal health.

When using a portable device such as a "boombox," placing it far from the teaching positing reduces the instructor's tendency to scream over the music. For example, speakers may be placed behind the students, facing the instructor, at the opposite end of the area. Figure 1 offers an example.

HOMEWORK SUGGESTION:

After a class that is cueing-intensive, consider planning some time for the voice to recover where you can be in silence, whenever possible. Additionally, sipping on cool water or other appropriate beverages and teas to promote throat health (available at most health food stores) will also help the throat recover from strong use. For more information on possible herbs and remedies, visit vocalist.org.uk. The National Institute of Health of the United States reports that long-term vocal overuse, especially without the assistance of a microphone, can yield to vocal nodules and even decrease overall vocal quality with age (NILM).

Because instructors often eat on the go, including while driving between classes and clubs, two nutritional issues arise. First, taking the time for proper nutrition becomes an issue. Second, because of the time crunch, the Slow Food Movement

Organization tells us that eating in a hurry not only prevents the body from extracting the total amount of calories from food, but it also can defeat the body's ability to enjoy the full *sensorial* approach to feeding (Dimoch).

HOMEWORK SUGGESTION:
When appropriate, take a moment to savor a snack. Eat in silence and in darkness for a few minutes because removing the other senses enhances awareness of taste buds. Try to chew each mouthful slowly until liqud. Commence with a single-flavor food, such as a piece of fruit of vegetable. Gradually work up to complex snacks. With each bite, savor each mouthful, asking yourself when was the last time you really tasted each ingredient in a snack, let alone an entire meal.

E is for EYES
The most commonly overlooked sense that instructors need to rest is sight. From the moment we press play, we scan our rooms constantly with keen eyes, unendingly evaluating the postures and movements of each class participant.

HOMEWORK SUGGESTION:
When not teaching, two simple daily exercises for eye health can work wonders to bring relaxation to both the eyes and the optic nerve. First, closing the eyes for two minutes refreshes the eye's functions. Additionally, slowly blinking the eyes for one

minute also rests the eyes. The *Journal of American Medical Association* (JAMA) reports that, if possible, doing both exercises in a dimly-lit area with only the light of a candle enhances the effectiveness of the second exercise (Rowe).

Additionally, proper headware during teaching may assist keeping the eyes void of dripping sweat and facial moisturizers that tend to flood the eyes with perspiration resulting from more intense movement.

E is for EARS

Some instructors describe music as the soul behind every group movement class. With the exception of mind-body disciplines, instructors often play loud music to create a sense of energy in the class. As effective as this is, a nasty cycle occurs. The louder the music in the area, the louder the instructor needs to cue in an effort to be heard. In addition to vocal strain, loud music taxes the ears. The BBC News reports that, when we fall into the habit of using our personal listening devices to listen to songs we use for work at the same volume, the tendency to adversely affect the health of the eardrums increases because we fail to let the eardrums relax (BBC).

Figure 1

XXXXXXXXXXXXXXXXX
XXXXXXXXXXXX
XXXXXXXXXX
XXXXXXX

--INSTRUCTOR HERE--

X = STUDENTS

 = MUSIC SPEAKERS

HOMEWORK SUGGESTION:

A 2004 JAMA study reported that, to avoid this fatigue, many Ear, Nose, and Throat doctors recommend not only listening to personal music at a lower volume than used classes, but listening to different types of music all together . This study reported that "having a softer volume for personal use music that is different from work music not only promotes ear healthy, but also helps to create a parasympathetic, relaxation response. If you play work music (to which you sweat and work out intensely) for personal time (where your body is more relaxed), it is quite possible for your body's systems (like heart rate) to speed up because of the physical association and "memory" of the work environment (Friedrich).

For this reason, some instructors do

not listen to work music on their personal time. June Kahn, 2009 IDEA Instructor of the Year Award Recipient, is the Life Power Pilates Coordinator for Lifetime Fitness in Colorado. She recommends "having a separate playlist for times when not working out. I use a relaxing playlist when driving between clubs to teach," she says, "because it keeps my body from staying in work mode. I also try to avoid ear buds and use a background stereo. At home, I relax with music that I would never use in class to create different types of subconscious associations between relaxation and my special music."

Long have scientists been interested in both the relaxing and healing powers of music, but only recently has science made headway at documenting its benefits. Known as "The Mozart Effect," the unique properties of music directly cause physiological and emotional responses in the body which can translate into changes in blood pressure, relaxation response, depth of breathing, different states of sleep, and, most interestingly, increased mental powers. Furthermore, the musical phenomenon of *entrainment* teaches us that a beating oscillator (such as the heart) will always try to beat at the rate of the other beats in its vicinity, meaning that the heart will always try to beat at the rate of the music it hears. Instructors knowing this can make sound choices to promote their own relaxation response and self-care (Levitin).

T is for TOUCH

Daily, instructors and trainers help others enhance their kinesthetic awareness. Unfortunately, hectic work schedules often prohibit that they, themselves, "check in" with their own. Classes like Feldenkrais offer a plethora of tips for instructors to help them learn how to take care of themselves through touch. This author schedules private Feldenkrais lessons with practitioner Valerie Grant (valeriecgrant@hotmail.com) randomly throughout the year to assess breathing, posture, and movement patterns. According to Grant, "Feldenkrais lessons promote self-care because they help instructors find greater ease and more efficient mobility for muscles. Patterns of habitual, unconscious muscle engagement lead to strain and injury, and Feldenkrais helps us discover our imbalances and learn to make movement choices that can prevent these parasitic patterns."

HOMEWORK SUGGESTION:

If finding a Feldenkrais practitioner does not prove possible for your, use touch to relax the body by practicing myofascial release. This is a gradual-to-deep self massage of muscle fascia and tissue that gets overworked as we teach and train. Start with a self-massage for five minutes of each foot. If you do not know how to massage the feet, just start with gentle squeezes all over the foot area for two minutes per foot. If possible, work up to using a foam ball or foam roller (available at power-systems.com) to massage muscles, release bands of collagen, and re-hydrate the muscles. For more information on this technique, consult meltmethod.com.

SMELL

Oftentimes in the gym environment, instructors face less-than-pleasant smells. Gym bags loaded with dirty clothes, car trunks, group fitness studios, chlorinated pool areas, and even locker rooms all sometimes offer unpleasant smells. Subconsciously via the sympathetic nervous system, the brain sends messages to the lungs to inhale and exhale less deeply to avoid the pungent odors. Donna Farhi, in *The Breathing Book*, reports that such hallow breathing can prevent the body from recovering sufficiently between classes because cells do not receive the proper amounts of oxygen they need to carry nutrients for repair. Consequently, overuse injuries, fatigue, and even insomnia can occur (Farhi).

HOMEWORK SUGGESTION:

Taking just a few steps to promote deep, conscious breathing between classes from aromatherapy can heighten one's recovery between workouts. Long known in the spa environment, the more pleasant the smell, the stronger the parasympathetic nervous system's role is to lengthen the inhalation and exhalation response. Examples of aromatherapy to induce a deeper breath response for instructors and trainers include:

- Lighting an aromatherapy candle when checking email at a desk area
- Placing an aromatherapy sachet into a backpack or gymbag
- Getting an ionizer for the car to neutralize smells and generate that "after-the-rain" fresh smell
- Creating an aromatherapy spray made of appropriate essential oils in a base of green tea for spraying on the chest and wrists between classes when taking a full shower isn't appropriate
- Adding a few drops of appropriate essential oils to give aromatherapy to after-shower moisturizing lotion or oil

Learning to practice self-care is crucial for today's versatile instructor and trainer. In our efforts to be versatile, often overlooked is our own health to rest as hard as we train. The homework suggestions in this article outline practical, quick, yet effective techniques for each of the five senses to assist instructors and trainers to stay healthy while giving so much service to others.

FREE! *For self-care vocal care video footage, check out "SPA FOR THE SOUL" under "HANDOUTS" under "FREE STUFF" at findLawrence.com*

Works Cited/References

BBC News. 2010. 9 May 2010 < http: //news.bbc.co.uk/1/hi/health/409987.stm>.

Dimock, Michael. "A Balancing Act" *The Slow Food Almanac.* Italy: Slow Food.com, 2008.

Farhi, Donna. *The Breathing Book.* New York: Henry Hold and Company, LLC: 1996.

Friedrich, M.J. Institute Probes Music's Therapeutic Potential. *Journal of American Medical Association.* April: 2004, 291:1554-1555.

Levitin, Daniel. *This is Your Brain on Music.* New York: Penguin, 2006.

NILM: National Institute on Health for Vocal Safety. nlm.nih.gov/medlineplus/throatdisorders.html.

Rowe, Susannah, and MacLean, Catherine. Preventing Visual Loss from Chronic Eye Disease in Primary Care. *Journal of American Medical Association.* March: 24/31, 2004; 291: 1487-1495.

LAWRENCE-isms

As a response to the number of requests I receive from attendees from all over the world for "something I said about..." or "the cute little rhyme about...," I am including here a non-exhaustive list of some of my most popular sayings and refrains from fitness over the past few years that I usually weave in some form or another into the experiences I create. These from part of my "first five minutes, last five minutes," and anywhere in between there is an appropriate opportunity.

When there are no quotation marks, these are my sayings. I attribute other quotes to their sources. Try to keep at least one saying prevalent in your mind that may be appropriate for each type of class you teach and use it.

- Limits? If you reach for the stars, all you get are the stars, but I've got a whole new spin: if you reach for the heavens, you get the stars thrown in.
- Dad said "we shouldn't stop playing because we are growing older because we will start growing old the moment we stop playing."
- The best teachers and trainers render themselves unnecessary.
- You found God? How wonderful for you....but God isn't lost.
- "Few of us plan to fail, but most of us fail to plan." Ben Franklin

- The world is round so you can't really see too far ahead of what's around the bend.
- How do you make God laugh? Tell her your plans for your life.
- Courage is fear you hold onto for a few moments longer.
- Try to find the eye of a hurricane and be still.
- Concentrate on the safety deposit box we call our bodies and take an inventory of the valuables you're keeping inside.
- Practice diligent joy.
- Laughing in yoga? It's okay to lighten up. We don't play "dead" until the very end in "corpse posture." The reason that angels can fly is that they take themselves so very lightly.
- We want to be consistently inconsistent in our training.
- The equipment you'll need today is an open mind, and open heart, and a willingness to train your five senses.
- If you don't stand for something, you'll fall for anything.
- We're not human beings having a spiritual experience because I believe we are spiritual beings right now having a human one.
- Fire yourself from the job of having to be manager of the universe.
- The most powerful words in the English language are "I AM."

- The pattern (movement) cannot be distant from the activity.
- Harness the power of intention and concentrate on _____.
- Draw yourself into your own silence.
- Smile in your feet, in your sitz bones, in your knees.
- Zen philosophy: you can't see yourself in running water; you have to be really still to see the reflection. If you are really really still in meditation you sit in a park and a bird will land on your head thinking you are an inanimate statue.
- Turn yourself inside out.
- Tell me HOW you teach, and I'll tell you WHAT it is that you are teaching.
- Take ownership of your (bodypart) _____.
- How would you teach if you knew they would love it?
- "It's amazing what you can do once you get out of your own way." P.L. Travers, author of *Mary Poppins*
- "There are no bad movements, just movements done badly." Molly Fox
- "I value only two things: wisdom and love. 'Wisdom' means that I'm wise enough to know that I don't know anything, and 'love' means that, with you around me, I have everything." Buddha
- "Activate your core; engage your pelvic floor." Gin Miller

- "If your brain conceives it and your heart believes it, your body will achieve it." Helen Vanderburg

SUGGESTED BIBLIOGRAPHY

Perhaps the best place to find free articles on a variety of group fitness and personal training topics is to check out the FREE STUFF at findLawrence.com. You will find there almost every article I've ever written for fitness. Under LINKS you will find fitness resources I believe are worthy.

Alter, M.J. *Science of Stretching.* Champaign, IL.: Human Kinetics Books, 1988.

ACE Fitness Matters. April/May: 2002, *citing Annual meeting of the Society for Neuroscience.* November 11, 2001. San Diego, California.

Biscontini, Lawrence. "Exercising Your Global Talents: Making the most of your ACE Faculty status." *ACE Faculty Network* Fall 5.3 (1999): 1-3.

Biscontini, Lawrence. "Fitness @ Your Fingertips." *Asiafit* May-June 2000: 32-34.

Biscontini, Lawrence. "Nothing Softer than the Water! What Mind-Body Hydro Classes Can Do For You." *The AKWA Letter Magazine* June-July 2000: 10-11.

Carrico, Maria. *Yoga Journals Yoga Basics: The Essential Beginners Guide to A Lifetime of Health and Fitness.* New York: Henry Holt, 1997

Castells, M. (2009). *Communication Power.* New York: Oxford University Press.

Cotton, Richard T., managing ed. *Personal Trainer.* California: American Council on Exercise (ACE), 2006.

Crompton, Paul. *The Elements of T'ai Chi.* Dorset, England: Element Books Limited, 1990.

Etnyre, B.R. "Antagonist muscle activity during stretching: a paradox re-assessed." *Medicine and Science in Sports and Exercise.* 1988 (20): 285-298.

Fox, Jenni, and Gould, Paul. *Yoga 101, a Practical and Fundamental Guide.* Avon Books, 1999.

Glisan, B. *The Spine in Sports* St. Louis, Mosby-Yearbook, Inc. *See especially pages 31-41 on treatment and prevention of athletic low back injuries with good general fitness information.*

Kendall, F.P., and McCreary, E.K. "Muscles and Testing Function. Baltimore: Williams & Wilkins, 1993.

Lund, Richard. *Wellness through T'ai Chi: Instruction in the Traditional Yang Style Taijiquan.* New Jersey: Woodbridge.

Mingwu, Zhang. *Chinese Oigong Therapy.* Jinan, China: Shandong Science and Technology Press, 1988.

Perrottet, Tony. *The Naked Olympics: the True Story of the Ancient Games.* New York: Random House, 2004.

Quinlan, P., Lane, J., Aspinall,L. "Effects of hot tea, coffee, and water ingestion on physiological responses and mood: the role of caffeine water and beverage type." *Psychopharmacology*, 34:2: 164-173, 1997.

Ricci, B. "Biomechanics of Sit-Up Exercises. *Medicine and Science in Sports and Exercise,* 1981, 13: 54-59.

ABOUT THE AUTHOR

—MINDFUL MOVEMENT & WELLNESS SPECIALIST AND SPA CONSULTANT—
Lawrence Biscontini, MA, CNC, personifies versatility in fitness and wellness education, and he has made fitness history by being the first fitness professional to receive the following awards: IDEA Association's Mind Body Visionary Presenter Award (2010), East Coast Alliance (ECA) Best All-Around Male Presenter (2010), ECA Presenter's Choice Premier Debut Award (2009), Athlie Clubs Japan Vote Lawrence's "Shakti" Program #1 (2008), Best Corporate Wellness Trainer for Xerox, Greece (2006), Best Mind-Body Presenter (ECA, 2005), Specialty Presenter of the Year Award (Can Fit Pro, 2004), Instructor of the Year Awards from IDEA (2004) and American Council on Exercise (ACE, 2002). In the summer of 2004, he participated in the Opening Ceremonies of the Athens 2004 Olympics with yoga and T'ai Chi. Lawrence served as the Wellness Consultant to the Golden Door Spa (goldendoorspa.com) chain for over ten years including the creation of the Golden Door in Puerto Rico under his direction where his award-winning programming at the Golden Door Spa received regular attention of both the press and the fitness & spa industry, such as in the April 2002 *Conde Nast* report ranking Lawrence's programming at Golden Door number 1 in the world. Large chains such as 24 Hour Fitness, Equinox (equinoxfitness.com), and Bally Total Fitness club chains call on Lawrence as Program Design Specialist to create some of their most exciting group fitness, mind-body, personal trainer, and aquatic programming, and, most recently, Lawrence is the Technical Director for yoga and T'ai Chi on the new fitwisetraining.com website. *Fitness Magazine (fitnessmagazine.com)* named Lawrence one of the Top Ten USA Trainers in 2003 (where he served on their Editorial Advisory Board from 2000-2007), and cast member clients of his from ABC's "General Hospital" in *ABC Soaps in Depth* magazine named Lawrence "fitness guru."

Possessing current ACE, AFAA, NASM, ACSM, AEA, Cooper CIAR, SCW-EDU, and Can-Fit-Pro personal trainer, group fitness instructor, and Nutritional Counselor certifications for land and aqua, Lawrence is a registered yoga teacher of Yoga Alliance and is a trainer for Beamfit, Reebok University, AFAA (International Certification Specialist), Resist-a-Ball, (resistaball.com), Gliding,™ Bender Ball, BOSU, and Power

254

Systems, and the American Red Cross as a volunteer CPR Instructor. Lawrence has created a signature experience called "Yo-Chi"® fusing yoga nad T'ai Chi, and has been seen on "LIVE with Regis and Kelly" and "CNN Headline News."

Most major certifying bodies and continuing education international providers and conventions count on Lawrence as faculty member, who not only trains the staff at other elite Golden Door Spas, but also travels as Spa & Fitness Consultant to help unique facilities and spas around the globe find an ideal blend of treatments, fitness, and wellness throughout its programs (Greenbrier, Canyon Ranch, Well Spa at Miramonte, among others).

Lawrence is also an author for such international fitness publications as the new Human Kinetics release *Morning Cardio Workouts* with June Kahn, AFAA's *Theory and Practice* industry standard textbook, and he contributes regularly to *AFAA's American Fitness* as a Contributing Writer, *ACE Faculty News*, *AKWA Newsletter Magazine, AsiaFit, SELF magazine,* among others. Lawrence's other books include *Running the Show: Excellence in Service* (customer service training for fitness professionals), *Cream Rises: Excellence in Private and Group Education* (teaching skills), *The One-Percent Factor: An Eccentric Unicorn's Approach to Touring and Traveling* as well as various texts on yoga, T'ai Chi, and Latin dance.

On an international scale, Lawrence serves on both IDEA Group Fitness & Steering Committees, Fitness Advisory Board for Fitness Magazine, and Faculty Advisory Board for the American Council on Exercise. For the fitness and consumer market, Lawrence appears in over 40 internationally-sold fitness videos and DVDs.

As Lawrence continues to inspire the world to fitness, he created various solutions to this end. First, FG2000 is a group of leading continuing education providers who offer accredited training at an international level in a variety of languages with a concentration on developing countries who otherwise would not be able to afford this training. For up-and-coming instructors, Lawrence established the Biscontini Scholarship to offer the opportunity for a promising instructor or personal trainer to attend the International World Fitness IDEA convention, SCW Fitness, and the East Coast Alliance on the east coast, yearly. He also began a NOTICE M.E.! program through which he helps empower instructors who have innovative ideas in the fitness industry.

Lawrence's mind-body study is extensive: with dual Master's Degrees in Spanish Literature & Translation and Education, and a minor in theology, he has studied *yoga* in India (2006) and in

255

the USA: at Kripalu Center in New York state with *yogis* from India, under Sri K. Pattabhi Jois (Ashtanga, India), Tias Little, Rodney Yee, Shiva Rea, Donna Rubin (Bikram, NYC), and Molly Fox. Lawrence is a registered Yoga Alliance teacher. Lawrence also has studied T'ai Chi under David Dorian-Ross, and Pilates under Lolita San Miguel (student to Joseph Pilates), June Kahn, Moira Stott, Elizabeth Larkham, and Leslie Bender. Lawrence studies Feldenkrais under John Link in NYC.

      Lawrence seeks community involvement via fitness. His company FG2000 takes premier fitness programming to developing countries with a non-for-profit mission, not to make money but to provide education. He founded a T'ai Chi Wellness group in Puerto Rico at a local church community, and continually teaches yoga to incarcerated teens in the Centro de Detención on the island. At the 2003 IDEA Convention, Lawrence helped raise over $3,000 for the National Aids Fund at an early morning charity workout, teaching both yoga and T'ai chi to fitness enthusiasts with friend Constance Towers from ABC's *General Hospital*. His cause of choice in the USA is to serve as spokesperson for the Sisters of Saint Joseph Villa based in Philadelphia, a retirement community where both Catholic religious sisters and lay community members alike find a home after a life of active service to others. In the spring of 2004, Lawrence brought fitness professionals together for the plight of New York City animals for the Broadway Barks foundation begun by friend Bernadette Peters (officialbroadwaybarks.org).

Lawrence served on the board for **Immunocise** in Dallas, Texas, and other organizations that use fitness to help those challenged in some way by HIV and AIDS. He has volunteered for **Workout for Hope**, and was the chief catalyst for Puerto Rico celebrating its first annual Workout for Hope in '98. In 2001, Lawrence initiated a "Fitness Unites" marathon in Puerto Rico to raise money for the **September 11th Fund**.

      Lawrence teaches in English, Spanish, Italian, and Greek, and is a resident of the world.
©2011

256